RECONNET TO LOVE

A Journey From Loneliness to Deep Connection

Yong Kang Chan

www.nerdycreator.com

Printed in the United States of America

First Edition, 2020

ISBN 978-981-14-6520-8

Cover illustrated by Rusty Doodle
Author photo by Benson Ang
Book edited by Jessica Bryan

CONTENTS

Part 3: Staying Connected

Preface

After recovering from depression in 2015, it took some time to regain my confidence in meeting new people. If you have read my memoir, *The Emotional Gift*, you know I had a couple of bad experiences in networking with entrepreneurs. These experiences brought out shame in me that I never knew existed. So when I went to my first social event in late 2017, after taking a two-year break, I was eager and apprehensive. A part of me wanted to reconnect with others. But at the back of my mind, there was also this nagging fear I might meet someone who would hurt me again. If it wasn't for the loneliness and boredom I was feeling from my lack of social contact, I probably wouldn't have gone out to meet new people.

Life is always miraculous. The more you don't want something to happen, the more the Universe brings it to you to help you grow. Little did I expect the first person I would meet would be Pat, who looked like James, my friend in secondary school who abandoned and betrayed me. Pat reminded me of James. They wear a similar type of glasses and share a tanned skin tone. It's not as though they look exactly the same or have the same personality. But when I first shook Pat's hand, I had a flashback of James, someone I had long forgotten and erased from my mind as a bad memory.

Initially, I didn't think too much about it. It's common for people to look alike, isn't it? So I brushed it aside. But after interacting with Pat for a few months, I noticed my fear of abandonment and betrayal starting to creep in again. I became uneasy, worried, and even angry when Pat took days to return my messages or didn't do what he had promised he would do. This was when I realized the Universe had other plans for me.

The people who hurt you the most are also the people who help you grow the most.

The Universe has been trying to help me let go of the hurtful stories I've been holding on to for so long. I have been given a chance to rewrite my past and resolve my issues with James through my new friendship with Pat. My past experiences have prevented me from staying open-hearted and truly connecting with the people I care about. They block me from receiving and giving love. Being disconnected from love, I'm bound to feel lonely.

So I am given a choice — to remain a victim of my past or set myself free, expand, and be the loving person I know I am. I chose the latter. This sets me on a quest to not only figure out how I can connect with others deeply, but more importantly, learn how to connect deeper with myself. I want to remove all the obstacles that cause my heart to close to other people. Hence, this book is born.

Reconnect to Love is the most difficult book I have written to date. I started writing in August 2018, but I was stuck for a very long time. It wasn't until November 2019, when a friend encouraged us to spend some time alone in a park, that I realized I needed to use a more spiritual approach. Writing this book has been a very humbling experience. I cried a lot of tears while processing my past experiences. It made me realize that even though I'm more self-compassionate now and healthy in many areas of my life, I'm still a victim when it comes to relationships. There is a lot of room for growth and expansion, and I'm grateful to be given this chance to learn and write about it.

As with my other books, most of the insights here are

drawn from my own experiences and observations. The names of the people I've written about have been changed to protect their identities. My writing is as simple as possible. If you are looking for something technical, complex, or extensively researched, this book might not be suitable for you. It's more suitable for readers who prefer self-reflection and learning from the experiences of other people.

Finally, a special mention to my readers who have shared with me how lonely they feel, and how much they desire deep connection, too. This book is especially for you!

With much love,
Yong Kang Chan
Singapore
2020

Loneliness Results From Our Disconnection to Love

"When you feel lonely, it's not because there are no other like-minded people for you to play with. It's because you have separated yourself from Who-You-Really-Are."

— ABRAHAM HICKS

Amy, an unpopular kid in school, is so blunt and negative that people don't like to be around her. When she posts something on social media, she eagerly waits for a like or a comment, but no one responds to her. She often compares herself to others on social media and wonders why they are more popular than she is. Amy saw photos of Belle's birthday party on social media, and felt excluded and rejected by her classmates because she wasn't invited to the party.

Candy, on the other hand, was invited to the party, but she was too shy to strike up a conversation with others during the party. Candy's only friend, Belle, was so busy playing the host that she had no time to talk with her. Everyone else seemed to be enjoying themselves so much and having such a fun time, chatting and laughing away. But she felt awkward. She didn't feel like she belonged in the group. Even though she was surrounded by many people and she's friendly and polite, she felt different from the rest.

After the party, Belle's mom cleaned up the mess while Belle wiped away her tears. The person she most wanted to be at the party, her dad, had not been there. He was on a business trip, again. Belle has a lot of friends but she doesn't feel close to any of them. She always pretends to be happy and positive around her friends because she wants them to accept her. Since Belle was young, her mom has taught her: *No one wants to be around someone who complains and whines.* So she was conditioned to believe she could not allow herself to be vulnerable in front of her friends. No one knows how she truly feels, not even her parents. She is lonely, too.

Belle's mom, Danni, is the perfect stay-at-home mom.

The family looks flawless on the outside—a loving couple with a bright daughter and a beautiful, posh home—but in reality, Danni's marriage is going through a rough patch. Her husband, Ethan, is often away on business trips and he has been working late for the past couple of years. He is hardly ever at home. Even when Ethan is home, he is cold and distant and they seldom speak openly with each other like they used to. Danni feels neglected by Ethan. She doesn't get it. She has done everything to please her husband, but yet he seems unappreciative. The toughest time for Danni is when Belle goes to school in the morning and she's left alone with a large, empty house and her imagination. She suspects Ethan is having an affair, but she doesn't want to confront him and risk ruining what's left of their relationship. Danni also doesn't want any of her friends to know she is worried, because she doesn't want to appear needy or less than perfect. She doesn't want to destroy the ideal family image she has built up over the years.

Ethan is an entrepreneur, but his business has been struggling recently. For the last couple of years, he has been working hard to get new clients and save his dying business. Being an entrepreneur can be lonely, at times. Even though he has employees, they rarely talk to him about anything other than work. As the leader, he has to make all the decisions, and sometimes his employees don't understand the big picture and why he operates the business the way he does. Also, Ethan feels he can't share his troubles with his wife or his friends. Since they are not entrepreneurs, he doesn't think they would be able to understand the hardships he is going through. Most of all, he doesn't want to disappoint Danni. She has not worked since she gave birth to Belle. He wants to continue to be the sole breadwinner of the family. Ethan believes he would feel worthless and not good enough for his spouse if he cannot support his family. Feeling stressed and disappointed with himself, he finds it hard to open up and talk to Danni.

Living miles away in another state is seventy-year-old, Fabian. He is Ethan's dad. Fabian's wife passed away and he has been living alone for the last five years. Ethan, his only child, hasn't contacted him in a while, and Fabian doesn't want to initiate contact either because they don't have a good relationship. Fabian has always been rather critical towards Ethan, and he knows Ethan doesn't like to be around him. But he can't help criticizing Ethan because he has such high expectations for his only son. Living alone, Fabian feels isolated and cut off from society. The only people he talks to are acquaintances in the grocery stores and the waiters at the restaurant where he eats his meals alone. His main companion is his television.

You might feel lonely, but you are not alone.

Everyone experiences loneliness, regardless of whether you are a teenager, a working adult, or a retiree. It doesn't matter whether you are single, attached or married, alone or with people, popular or unpopular, everyone feels lonely from time to time when we are disconnected from our spiritual self.

From a spiritual perspective, we are love. Our true essence is that of love. We are inseparable from love. There is also no separation between others and us because we are one. We are always connected through this universal source of love. Love is always present within us and around us.

However, from a psychological perspective, our mental perceptions and beliefs can create separation and cause us to disconnect from the source of love that is always within us. When Amy *thinks* other people don't like to be around her, she's disconnected. When Candy *thinks* she's an outcast, she's disconnected. When Belle *thinks* her dad loves his work more than her, she's disconnected. When Danni *thinks* her husband is cheating on her, she's disconnected. When Ethan *thinks* no one will understand what he's going through, he's disconnected. When Fabian *thinks* his son doesn't want to speak to him, he's also disconnected.

Whether what you think is true or not, the moment you *believe* the story your ego tells you about how separated you are from other people, there will be a disconnection from the love within and you will feel lonely.

Love Is Always Available to Us From Within

Most of us think love comes from outside of us. We believe our lack of love creates our loneliness. So if we receive love, attention, or companionship from someone else, we believe we will feel less lonely. The truth is that love is always available to us from within.

When we feel lonely, we are not lacking in love.
We are disconnected from love.

Disconnection doesn't mean love is not available to us. It's the other way round. We are not available to receive the love from deep within us. We pay so much attention to our mental chatter that we shut the door to love and no love and warmth can flow inside us. Our bodies feel cold and constricted.

Let me use an analogy to illustrate this idea. When an electrical appliance is unplugged from the socket, we can't use the appliance anymore. It doesn't mean electricity isn't available. It just means the appliance is disconnected from the source of electricity. We need to plug the electronic appliance back into the socket to get the electricity flowing, which will allow the appliance to work again. Likewise, when you feel lonely, you are disconnected from the source of love, but love is not absent. Love is always available to you at all times. You just have to reconnect to the love within.

Seeking love from someone else is like going to their house and using their electricity. Yes, you can use their electricity *if they allow you to.* But what if they are not at home? What if they are not even aware of their electrical source and cannot consciously give you what you want? Isn't it easier to use the electricity in your own home? After all, you have direct access to it.

We share the same source of love as other people in the same way we share the same electrical supply in our house.

Whatever other people have, we have within us, too. If not, where do you think the people who shower you with love and attention get their love from? When we are overwhelmed with loneliness, the best way is to insert our plug back to the socket and reconnect to our own internal source of love.

About This Book

Friends can provide us with love and support. But this book is not about making friends or building better relationships with others. This book is about clearing the psychological obstacles that prevent us from feeling connected to others in the first place. It's about shifting our perspective from the mental to the spiritual. By changing or removing the stories that our egos tell us, we become closer to the love we are meant to be.

The information in this book cannot help you get rid of loneliness, but it *can* help you embrace solitude and face loneliness when you experience it. Solitude can be good for spiritual growth, but people tend to confuse it with loneliness. So in the beginning, I discuss the differences between solitude and loneliness. You will learn how you are conditioned to feel lonely and the subtle things you do to avoid loneliness. In Chapter 3, you will come to understand the larger purpose of loneliness, and why feeling lonely isn't something you should avoid. I also discuss what to do when you feel lonely.

Part 2 of the book goes deeper into the causes of our ongoing disconnection. The focus here is on the "story structure" the ego uses to keep us disconnected from love and other people. Part 2 also explores some of our common past experiences, beliefs, and habits to help us understand how they add to the story built by the ego.

Finally, in Part 3, there are some questions to help you self-reflect and rewrite your ego's stories. The nature of love—what it is and what it is not—is discussed from a spiritual perspective, and how you can practice solitude to deepen your connection to love. After going deep, we end the book by going broad. In the last chapter, there are some suggestions to help you connect better with others from a place of love and spirituality.

So now, let's begin by understanding the difference between solitude and loneliness.

PART 1

Facing Loneliness

Chapter 1

The Confusion Between Solitude and Loneliness

"Loneliness and solitude are two different things. Solitude is better for us, as it means being alone without feeling lonely."

— ELIF SHAFAK, THE FORTY RULES OF LOVE

After being a tutor for two years, I started to feel isolated. Although I enjoy working alone and the freedom I get from my job, it has somewhat affected my social life. My friends hardly contact me anymore because I usually have lessons at the times when they are free.

At first, I thought I would feel much better if I took the initiative and reached out to my friends. But after getting in touch with some of them, I realized we had gradually grown apart because of the choices we made. I'm self-employed, but most of them are employees, working in a corporation. I'm single, but most of them are married and have kids. My friends don't understand what I do as an author and why I choose to write books. On the other hand, I don't fully understand what it's like to be a parent, and I no longer share the same struggles they have working as an employee.

More importantly, after recovering from depression, I was not the same person I used to be. I'm in a much different place psychologically and spiritually. My priorities, values, and interests have changed quite drastically. When I meet up with people I used to be close to, I don't feel close to them anymore, and I know I have to make new friends.

So at the end of 2017, I started attending social events again to meet like-minded others. I joined groups of people who have personalities and interests similar to mine. It was great at the beginning, but after a while, I felt something was missing. With most people, I still don't feel the deep connections I desire. Also, some of the people I feel a deep connection with don't seem to be interested in developing a closer bond with me.

Loneliness is a journey we have to walk alone.

Our inner disconnection cannot be resolved

by external connections.

After two more years of seeking, I finally realized loneliness is not due to a lack of external connection. It's a result of internal disconnection. We feel lonely because we have lost our alignment with the love and abundance within. We are, first and foremost, disconnected from our true selves. This, in turn, causes us to feel disconnected from other people.

Most of us falsely believe that when we interact with others, make more friends, or find a soulmate, our feelings of loneliness will dissipate. But this doesn't work, because being alone is not the cause of our loneliness. We feel lonely because of our insatiable desire for deep connection and ideal relationships. So even when we have a loving and supportive friend or partner by our side, we are still disappointed because we are focused on what's missing in our relationships. Our disconnection with other people is secondary to the emptiness we feel inside. At best, people can relieve our loneliness temporarily. But the lonely feeling will soon come back if our internal disconnection persists.

Being Alone vs. Feeling Lonely

Being alone is not the same as feeling lonely although it's easy to confuse the two. First, there is a difference between *feeling* and *being*. Loneliness is the feeling of lack. You feel like something or someone is missing from your life. It's as though no one cares about you, no one gets you, no one supports you, and no one has the same experiences as you do. It's also a feeling of disconnection, isolation, separation, and the yearning for more. More often than not, this feeling of loneliness is created by your thoughts and beliefs. Solitude, being alone, on the other hand, is merely a state of being within yourself. They are not mutually inclusive.

You can be alone and not feel lonely at all,

or you can feel very lonely

even when you are with many people.

For instance, when you are meditating, you can be physically alone and yet feel very connected with yourself, the people around you, and the world. You can also travel alone and find a lot of freedom and joy in it. Solitude can help us process our emotions, become more self-aware, and go deeper into our spiritual essence. It can be beautiful, especially if you choose to be alone.

On the other hand, married and dating couples are not immune to loneliness. They can feel lonely in their marriage and relationships, too, if they feel a *lack* of emotional connection with their partner. Also, being in groups doesn't always make us feel like we belong. Some of us feel worse when we are surrounded by other people and we realize none of them understand us. It just reminds us of how much we don't fit in.

Often, what bothers us is not solitude but how we think others will perceive us when we are alone. Some activities such as watching a movie or eating can be done alone, but yet we feel uncomfortable doing them in public because we are afraid of being judged by others. Doing things alone in public makes us look like losers who have no friends. Even if we have to eat alone in public, some of us use our mobile phones and pretend we are busy at work, or we text someone to minimize the judgment we imagine others have about us.

Our own judgment about being alone evokes our feeling of loneliness. We believe being alone is bad or less desirable than being in a group or a pair. So when we walk alone in the street and see dating couples or a group of people, we feel bad about ourselves and wish we had someone alongside us, so we wouldn't feel we are lacking. However, there is a subtle difference here. It's not our state of being alone that causes us to feel lonely. It's our negative perception of being alone. If you are alone and you are fine with it, then there is only solitude. Loneliness only comes when you are dissatisfied with being alone.

How We Become Afraid and Ashamed of Being Alone

Once my student, Jade, asked me, "Are you married?"

"Nope, I'm single," I replied.

She exclaimed, "That's so sad!"

I was taken aback by her huge reaction, and I thought to myself, *Since when is being single a miserable state of being?*

Since I was young, I have always been more introverted. I enjoy spending time alone and doing my own thing. Being alone doesn't bother me much. In fact, it energizes me and makes me feel recharged. So I asked Jade why she thinks being single is sad. She said her family keeps telling her to get married. They said if she doesn't get married, she will be lonely when she gets old. Even though my student is only sixteen years old, I'm amazed by how much pressure she receives from her parents to start her own family.

But she's not the only one. My brothers and I are often pressured by our parents to find a girlfriend and get married. Our father, in particular, reminds us of how miserable we will be if we don't have children to support us when we are old. He says we are foolish not to plan for a family.

From the time we are young,

our families and society give us the message that

it's not acceptable to be alone.

It's not normal to be single. Being alone is scary. You will feel lonely if you don't get married. Loneliness is bad. No one can cope with loneliness. We should do our best to avoid it. We are incomplete and inadequate if we are by ourselves. We need others to make us feel whole and complete.

Even if they don't say it aloud, our parents unconsciously project their fear and shame about being alone onto us. We are also conditioned by society to find a partner, get married, and start a family. Whether we have the desire or not, this is the societal norm and we feel judged when we deviate from the norm.

Once a reader told me she wants to have a partner and children but she feels rather depressed. She thinks it's not going to happen because she is getting old. Out of curiosity, I asked her why she wants to start a family. Initially, she told me that she wants to procreate, be intimate, and share her life with somebody. But as I delved deeper, she said she hates being alone all the time. She feels as though she is being looked down on. People have been asking her when she is going to find a boyfriend and get married, because she's in her forties and it's getting too late to have children. That's when I realized her desire to be accepted and approved by others is much stronger than her desire to have a partner. She's not getting a partner to experience a loving relationship. She's getting a partner to stop others from judging her.

It's the same with my dad. When I probed further, I realized his actions are the result of social pressure and shaming. His friends brag about the number of grandchildren they have and shame him for being a bad parent who doesn't know how to teach his kids to start a family. He feels judged, and this is why he needs to constantly remind us to get married.

Due to the social stigma around being single and alone, some of us get attached to another person or join a community hastily just to avoid being judged. But in doing so, we can end up with an unhappy marriage or unhealthy friendships. More importantly, we sacrifice our emotional integrity for social acceptance.

Is Your Loneliness a Result of Social Conditioning?

When you feel lonely, can you tell whether the emotion arises authentically, or is it heavily influenced by beliefs you have adopted from society? In other words, is your feeling of loneliness a result of not meeting other people's expectations? Do you feel unfulfilled because society tells you so?

The issue with adhering to societal norms is that we lose touch with our true desires and emotions. We don't know how we feel anymore and we don't know what we want. We rely on society and other people to tell us how we *should* feel and what we *should* desire. We adopt the collective beliefs of society without doubting whether these beliefs are true or not for us. For example, our beliefs might include:

- *Being alone will make you feel lonely.*
- *Getting married is better off than staying single.*

- *If you are single, then something must be wrong with you.*
- *It feels pathetic to dine, go to the cinema, or travel by yourself.*
- *Once you find a partner, you won't be lonely.*
- *Having an active social life will make you feel fulfilled and connected.*

Even though your friends and family might be well-intentioned, they are sharing with you what *they* believe will cause *them* to feel lonely and how *they* cope with it. But no one can tell you exactly how you should feel and what to desire. Just because others feel lonely when they are alone doesn't mean you will, or that you *should* feel the same way. Just because someone wants to get married and have children doesn't mean you need to. And just because someone doesn't know how to deal with loneliness doesn't mean you can't cope with it. These are their beliefs, not yours.

Emotions are supposed to be subjective and felt in the moment. Yet, we allow others to determine how we should feel.

Instead of allowing our emotions to arise naturally as and when they occur, we use conditions that we have adopted from society to predetermine our emotions. *If we do this, we will feel lonely. If we do that, we will not feel lonely.* But these predetermined emotions are inauthentic. Not only are they based on other people's opinions, but we also tell ourselves how we should feel in a given situation, instead of allowing ourselves to feel what we are really feeling. Emotions don't work like a mathematical formula or a programming code: *If you do A, you will definitely get B.* It's not always that straightforward. The truth is, for some of us, even if we achieve the goals we set out to attain, we still won't feel what we *think* we should feel. Every context is unique. Sometimes, you might feel lonely when you are alone, while other times you might not. It usually depends on what you are thinking at the moment. You can't plan your emotions.

But when we adopt these societal rules and conditions, we end up feeling lonely more often than is necessary. We create unnecessary stress, resistance, and anxiety for ourselves. We think we need to create certain conditions before we can feel happy. And when we don't, we feel awful—like my reader, who felt lonely and depressed because she believes she has to get married and have children by a certain age. People who are single and of the same age but who don't have these societal beliefs, are more at peace than she is because they don't feel the pressure to get married.

Emotions such as loneliness give us valuable insights. But there is a difference between the loneliness you feel in the moment and the loneliness you tell yourself you *should* feel because you are lacking in some way. When we focus on meeting social conditions, rather than tuning in to our internal guiding system, we mess up the information provided by that system and we don't get an accurate read about how we truly feel. Instead, we confuse what we want with what society wants from us, and we train ourselves to meet other people's expectations.

Our protection against loneliness is exactly what keeps the loneliness intact.

Furthermore, when we are conditioned to be afraid of loneliness and believe that it is bad for us, we fail to see its purpose. We develop strategies to avoid loneliness and structure our lives around loneliness. Feeling lonely at home on Friday nights? Go to the bar. All by yourself? Call a friend. Your friends are not available? Watch television, surf the Internet, or find something else to occupy yourself. Whether the strategies we adopt are positive or negative is beside the point. Instead of living the life we want, we live a life designed to *prevent* us from the feelings *we don't want.* When we don't accept and embrace our feelings, we just keep repeating the same old habits that perpetual our loneliness, which only moves us further away from love — not closer to love.

Chapter 2

How We Escape From Loneliness

"The spiritual task is not to escape your loneliness, not to let yourself drown In it, but to find its source."

— HENRI NOUWEN, THE INNER VOICE OF LOVE

In October 2018, after my students had completed their examinations, I had no more lessons for the rest of the year. Initially, I thought it would be a good time to spend some quiet time alone to recharge and write this book. However, as the holiday approached, I had other thoughts.

One night, I found myself planning a grand, one-month holiday. I was browsing a website called *Worldpackers*, a platform that allows people to exchange their time for accommodation and food in another country. I was attracted to a great hostel in Bangkok, Thailand called *The Yard* and excited about the possibilities. It had the family vibe and sense of belonging I yearned for. There was a cooking class on Monday, outdoor movie screening on Wednesday, acoustic music on Friday, and yoga on Saturday—all the things I love to do. Furthermore, they were looking for a writer for their blog. I could trade my writing skills for a month of accommodation in the hostel. I would also be given days off to travel around Bangkok, a city I had never been to before. What a great experience it would be! I almost applied, but then I had a realization:

Everything seemed perfect,

except I was running away from loneliness.

For the previous couple of months, I had been so busy helping my students with their examinations that I hadn't been socializing. When I first discovered The Yard online, I was already conjuring up fantasies in my mind. Looking at the reviews and photos, I fantasized about how meaningful my experiences would be, and how nice it would be to meet new friends and be close to them. I imagined we would become lifelong friends, like family, and finally I would belong to a group. My mind even persuaded me the experience would inspire me to write this book, because I would discover what it is like to not feel lonely anymore.

But after I became more grounded, I realized my mind was at the hostel even before I was physically there. Contrary to what my mind told me, it's unlikely there would be time to sit down quietly and write a book while also interacting with other people and working for them. Plus, I could see the same old pattern my mind was creating. My mind has the habit of idealizing relationships and fantasizing about the future. By having so many expectations about the trip, I was already setting myself up for disappointment. There have been many times in the past when I thought I had finally found a group that could give me a sense of belonging, but I would end up feeling I didn't fit in. I had some deep-seated beliefs that were causing this disconnection. But instead of addressing the issue and my lonely feelings, my mind always sets up such wonderful, ideal scenarios of what something could be. Then when things don't go as imagined, my inner critic comes in and says: *Told you so. No one likes you. You don't fit in anywhere.* And I feel bad about myself again.

The way many of us cope with loneliness is to run away from it.

Instead of addressing our emotions directly, our minds are always looking for the next thing to fill up our time and attention so we don't have the space to feel lonely. But the relief these activities offer is only temporary. They are quick fixes that numb our painful emotions. Similar to painkillers, once the effects wear off the lonely feelings come back again. Then we have to keep relying on these activities to keep us occupied. If we are not careful, we can become addicted to the activities. This, in turn, creates another set of problems we must deal with. Furthermore, when we don't deal with our feelings when they first arise, we allow them to intensify and grow in momentum. Once loneliness becomes chronic, it is much harder to deal with than when it first surfaces.

In this chapter, we will explore the four things we commonly do to escape from loneliness so you can catch yourself before you avoid your emotions.

Fantasy: Using Illusions to Feel Connected

Fantasizing or idealizing is a strategy I frequently use to cope with loneliness. Growing up, I would play and talk to my toys by myself. They were my imaginary friends. These fantasies compensated for my lack of social and emotional connections at the time. But even now, it's still my habit to have conversations with other people in my head.

Fantasy gives us the illusion we are loved and connected to others. When we fantasize, we don't usually notice we are feeling lonely, because we are preoccupied with the positive images in our minds. Fantasizing is a self-soothing technique that children use to provide immediate relief from discomfort. As children, we use our imagination to protect ourselves from emotional pain and difficult situations, such as neglect, abandonment, abuse, and other traumas. Being small and powerless, there's nothing much we can do to get out of troubling situations except imagine a better scenario. Fantasizing that our parents or someone else out there loves us can help soothe our separation anxiety and disconnection.

As adults, some of us still use this same technique. When we want to get closer to someone but we don't believe we can, we create an illusion to ease the powerlessness we feel. We imagine ourselves in a romantic relationship or think we are close to others so we can escape from our feelings of loneliness. Sometimes, we also imagine we are special, well-liked, and popular among our peers and how we are admired by them. This gives us a false sense of desirability and belonging. Plus, it's easy and fun to fantasize. In a blink of an eye, we can get everything we want in our fantasies without having to do anything. We are in control of our imagination. Everyone in our dreams obeys us, and we feel powerful.

However, whenever we compare our imagination with reality, we are often disappointed. People are usually not as loving as we imagine them to be. We can't control others and make them behave in real life like they do in our fantasies. More importantly, it reminds us that we can't have what we want, we are flawed in certain ways, or we are not as desirable and significant as we think we are.

Fantasizing from time to time is harmless.
But don't use an imagined closeness as a substitute for real intimacy.

Over-fantasizing can get in the way of authentic connections. When we idealize others, we don't see them for who they are. Instead of spending time getting to know another person, we spend time in our minds. We think we are in love with someone, but we are actually in love with the perfect image our minds have created of the other person.

Furthermore, there is no risk to fantasizing. We can be

close to someone and that person will never reject us. It allows us to pretend we are in a loving relationship with someone, while maintaining an emotional distance from that person and ourselves. But this emotional distance is precisely what makes some of us feel lonely in the first place. By not being open and true about our emotions, our relationships lack depth.

Authentic connections require us to be open and vulnerable. Doing so means we have to first explore and be in touch with ourselves and then share our deepest thoughts and feelings with another person. This is risky because people might judge and reject us, or they might not want to hear us talk about our feelings. But this is where the real, meaningful connection with others often lies.

Dependency: Relying on Others for Love and Company

Another thing we commonly do to escape from loneliness is to depend on others. I used to have this friend in school who wanted a companion for everything he did. Even though we didn't talk much when we studied, he felt more comfortable when he was studying with someone else. Before loneliness can even show up, he made sure there were people around him that he could talk to.

As children, we are trained to believe in the power of others. Growing up, we depend on our parents and caretakers for love, food, shelter, and everything else. By the time we reach adulthood, we will have learned how to take care of our own physical needs. But when it comes to emotional needs, most of us pass this responsibility from our parents to our friends, and then to our spouse.

We are constantly looking to others for love,

support, and happiness,

not realizing that the best person

to meet our emotional needs lies within us.

When we transfer our responsibilities to others, we also unknowingly give our power away to others and create dependencies. We need other people to be there for us so we don't feel lonely. We need the validation and attention of other people, before we can allow ourselves to believe we are lovable and good enough. When people distance themselves from us, we start to feel insecure and cling onto them. Instead of taking care of our own emotions, our emotional state is very dependent on what other people do or don't do. In a way, we are still children, powerless and looking to others to help us take care of our emotions.

It's great to have emotional support and love from your friends and family, but if we keep running to them whenever we feel lonely, we won't develop the skills we need to cope with our own emotions. More importantly, we reaffirm that love comes from the outside, and we lose sight of the love that is always within us.

In extreme cases, some of us are so afraid of feeling lonely that we stay in any relationship. Some of us would rather jump from relationship to relationship, or remain in unhealthy relationships we know aren't good for us, than to stay single. We have become so dependent on others that we find it difficult to function in the world on our own without feeling lonely.

Divergence: Focusing on Others Instead of Yourself

Instead of attending to our own emotions and acknowledging how we feel, some of us ignore loneliness by focusing on other people and their problems. Doing so takes the attention away from us and keeps us occupied. When we fret about other people's problems, we have no time to think about our own problems. It distracts us from our unpleasant emotions, and we don't realize how lonely we actually feel because we are busy taking care of others.

This is also a learned behavior that is passed down from generation to generation. From a young age, most of us are taught to please others and put other people's needs above our own. We are praised when we do what our parents want. But if we don't do what we are told, our parents might become unhappy with us or scold us. To be loved by our parents, we learn to please them and neglect our desires in the process. Our feelings and desires become less important compared to others. So when we grow up, our emotions are often not a priority. Instead, we scan the environment for problems that others might have and readily offer our help.

It's less painful to fix the problems of others than to fix your own.

However, if we ignore our feelings and focus too much on others, we begin to lose touch with our feelings. We lack emotional boundaries and we can be easily affected by others. When other people are happy, we are happy. When they are sad, we are sad. It becomes more difficult for us to differentiate our feelings from those of other people.

Some of us become codependent. We feel a compulsive need to be needed. We keep worrying about other people's problems and believe they cannot resolve them without our help. So we keep taking care of them at the expense of ourselves, and we burn ourselves up in our relationships. It becomes difficult to break away from dysfunctional relationships and stop supporting harmful behaviors because our sense of identity depends on how much others need us.

In the end, both parties in the relationship will not be able to grow. There is no incentive for the dependent person to change, because he can rely on the codependent person to do everything for him. He knows that no matter what he does or how hurtful he behaves, the codependent person will not leave him. The codependent person, on the other hand, might feel resentful for over-extending himself, while subconsciously he can't afford the dependent person becoming more self-sufficient. If the dependent person grows and becomes self-sufficient, how can the codependent person meet his *need to be needed*? So once two people are stuck in this type of pattern, they are likely to maintain the status quo.

Numbing: Using Substances and Activities to Avoid Feeling Pain

Numbing is something we do unconsciously. When we feel shame, sadness, fear, stress, or other painful emotions, we tend to numb them out with substances and activities. Loneliness is one of the emotions we frequently numb to avoid feeling. Whenever we feel lonely, some of us reach for a cigarette, a glass of wine, or a tub of ice cream. Others keep themselves busy with work or recreational activities such as shopping, watching videos, and gaming.

Nowadays, it's easy to numb ourselves because there are so many sensory pleasures and activities available to consume and participate in. Sometimes, we engage in these activities with others to give ourselves a false sense of belonging. For example, people go for a smoke break together or they drink alcohol socially to try to fit in and feel more accepted and relaxed around others.

When we numb our pain,

we also numb our joy.

On the surface, it seems like nothing is wrong with self-indulgence. But when we keep using various activities to numb our emotional pain, we don't feel the joy from our activities anymore. Numbing doesn't just reduce the intensity of our unpleasant emotions, it dulls our positive emotions, our joy and our passion. Rather than enjoying life, we end up feeling like robots that keep repeating the same things over and over.

Furthermore, some of the substances and activities we indulge in are highly addictive, even though they might appear to be harmless or even desirable, at first; for example, exercising, working, and the use of social media and smartphones to connect with others. By doing the same things repeatedly, we train ourselves to rely on these substances and activities. Once our minds associate comfort with them, breaking away can be a challenge. We can't put these substances or activities aside without feeling a compulsive need to use or do them. Also, once we start to have a higher tolerance for addictive activities, we have to amp them up to get the same effects and comfort they bring.

Once numbing becomes our habitual way of dealing with loneliness, we don't even feel our loneliness anymore. We automatically reach for the things that provide us comfort and we can't stop, because once we stop, all the emotions we have been avoiding will show up.

How to Catch Yourself Avoiding Loneliness

We avoid loneliness more often than we realize. Nowadays, everybody seems very busy, but if you ask yourself, "What am I busy with?", you might find that most of the things you do are not important. They are only useful in hiding your loneliness.

To catch yourself avoiding loneliness, pause frequently and check how you are feeling. Pay special attention to the times when you are using technology. It's easy to go unconscious when we use technology. Ask yourself, *Do I really enjoy doing this?* There is nothing wrong with enjoying a good movie or browsing the Internet if that is your intention. But we often allow our minds to go on autopilot, and we continue to do things even when we have lost interest in them. Sometimes, we do things automatically without realizing we are using these activities to distract ourselves from feeling and thinking. So it's a good habit to pause, observe what you are doing from time to time, and check to see whether you are avoiding your emotions.

Another way to find out whether you are avoiding your feelings is to sit down for a few minutes and *do nothing.* Not doing anything includes not fantasizing about the future, ruminating about the past, or thinking about anything. It really means doing nothing. Just follow your breath and notice your body as it expands and contracts. After a while, your mind might start to suggest some activities. Write them down. They are what you normally use to avoid feeling your emotions.

When you understand how you escape from loneliness, the next time you are involved in an activity, ask yourself, *Am I running from an emotion? Do I really want to do this?* before you decide whether to continue the activity, or not.

Chapter 3

What to Do When You Feel Lonely

"Loneliness, when accepted, becomes a gift that will lead us to find a purpose in life."

— PAULO COELHO

Loneliness seldom comes alone. It is usually accompanied by other emotions. For instance, shame comes into play when we justify the reasons we are alone and feel excluded. We think perhaps we are unlovable and not good enough for other people.

This is why one person's experience with loneliness can be different from another person's. It's also difficult to tell which emotion came first—loneliness or another emotion, because they usually feed off each other. Someone who feels depressed often feels lonely, too, because they tend to isolate themselves from other people, thinking no one will understand what they are going through. On the other hand, someone who suffers from chronic loneliness can become depressed when they feel hopeless about their situation and don't believe their life will improve.

So when we resist loneliness, we aren't just avoiding loneliness. We are usually avoiding some of the following emotions that commonly show up, along with loneliness:

- **Shame:** This feeling tells us what aspects of ourselves are unworthy of love. When we feel ashamed, we either hide these aspects of ourselves or distance ourselves from others. But this only makes us lonelier.

- **Fear:** We are afraid of being isolated, abandoned, or excluded by others. So we people-please and change ourselves to fit in with others, only to realize we have abandoned our true essence in the process and we feel lonelier than ever.

- **Grief:** Losing someone significant in our life can make us feel lonely. The person who has been keeping us from feeling lonely is gone. It feels as if no one else can ever replace this special person in our hearts.

- **Anxiety:** Loneliness can trigger a lot of anxiety when we feel people are distancing themselves from us. We can also feel helpless and unprotected when we are on our own.

- **Despair:** Losing hope in finding intimacy and meaningful connections prolongs the feeling of loneliness. You feel so disconnected from the world and everyone else that life seems meaningless.

- **Rejected:** We want to be accepted by a group or be loved by someone, but the feelings are not mutual and not reciprocated. So we feel disconnected and unwanted by others.

- **Envy:** When we see other people who are happy together, and we are not part of a group or a relationship like they are, we sometimes feel envious. The happiness of others reminds us of what we don't have and how lonely we are.

- **Misunderstood:** We might have many friends who know us on a superficial level but they don't know us deeply enough. Sometimes, it can also feel isolating, or like everyone is against us, when we feel misunderstood.

To reach the love deep within, the emotions hiding

inside our bodies need to be brought to the surface, expressed, and released, even though the mind will try to escape from pain. We need to rewire the mind so that we don't perceive processing emotion as painful. In fact, it can be rewarding when we understand the deeper purpose of our emotions.

The Purpose of Loneliness

Loneliness has a purpose, like other emotions. Its purpose is to remind us to reconnect to the deepest part of ourselves, which is pure love. It shows us that at a particular moment in time we are disconnected from our hearts and love.

Feeling lonely is the same as feeling thirsty, hungry, and tired—in the sense that when you feel thirsty and hungry, you drink water and eat food. When you are tired, you sleep. Thirst, hunger, and tiredness are signals from your brain telling you that you need replenishment. Feeling lonely is the signal you have lost connection. Loneliness is not as life-threatening or bad as our minds exaggerate it to be. Like thirst and hunger, we don't die from it the instant we notice we feel lonely.

Loneliness is simply a reminder we are disconnected. There is nothing negative about loneliness.

If you are disconnected from something, simply find a way to reconnect. When an electrical appliance isn't working, we don't label it as damaged and buy a new one immediately, do we? We check to see if it's connected with an electrical source. If it isn't, we insert the plug into the socket to see if the appliance will work properly. It's the same with loneliness. There is no need to run away from loneliness the instant we feel lonely. We can check our connection first and see if we have any thoughts or mental stories that are causing us to lose our connection with love.

Rather than having this adverse relationship with loneliness, know that loneliness is there to provide us with valuable information. It points out the beliefs, perceptions, and stories that are blocking us from having a deep connection with Source (Spirit) and other people. Having an awareness of these patterns and triggers can help us change habitual behaviors that no longer serve us.

Overcoming loneliness is not about getting rid of it forever. It's about accepting the purpose of loneliness.

We will still feel lonely from time to time, but this is a good thing. It shows us that our internal guidance system is functioning properly. Imagine your body is dehydrated, but there is no signal to tell you that you are thirsty, and you end up dying before you can find water. Loneliness is an indicator that love is not flowing in our bodies and we are disconnected from our true essence. Without this internal guidance system, you will not be aware you are disconnected and you won't do anything to reconnect.

Loneliness doesn't kill us unless we allow ourselves to stay in a lonely state for too long. To resist loneliness is to ignore the signs our internal guidance system gives us. It's like knowing we are thirsty but we don't drink water, or we know we are tired but we don't allow ourselves to rest. If we can recognize the message that loneliness brings and embrace its purpose, loneliness can be very helpful for our growth.

How to Feel Your Painful Emotions

Recognizing the purpose of loneliness is the first step in embracing loneliness. But what do you do when loneliness or other painful emotions arise and you want to run away from them? Here are the steps you can follow.

1. Stop whatever you are doing immediately.

The moment you realize you feel lonely or you don't feel good, just stop everything you are doing immediately. The next step varies depending on what you are doing when you have this awareness.

If you realize you are doing something to avoid feeling lonely, or an activity is making you feel lonely, get up and go to a quiet place where you can be alone and free of this simulation. So, for example, if you have a desire to text someone or check what other people are doing on social media, put down your phone and physically move to somewhere else. A change of environment can help stop an urge to take a particular action.

If you realize you are lost in your head and fantasizing about a relationship or ruminating about how lonely you feel, immediately shift your attention from your mind to your body or something else in the external environment. If you are lying down, sit up straight and choose a body part, such as your foot, and put all your attention on it. Alternatively, you might choose to focus on something external such as the trees outside your window, or you could look around your room and observe your surroundings. By shifting your attention to something tangible, you are shifting your attention from the interpretations in your mind to pure sense perception. This can reduce your thoughts and help you snap out of repetitive, thinking loops.

2. Direct your attention to your body.

After you break away from your activities and thoughts, observe how your whole body is feeling, in the moment.

- Does your chest feel tight?
- Do your hands and feet feel cold?
- Do you feel like crying?
- Does your body feel tense?
- Are any of your limbs shaking?
- Is there shortness of breath?

You can close your eyes if it helps you feel your body. Also, notice if there is an urge to move away from an unpleasant feeling. For example, you might try to shift your attention back from your body to your mind. You might start to fantasize or go back to the activity you were previously doing. Alternatively, you might feel numbness or a tingling sensation throughout your body. Detachment from your body might have become your habitual way of avoiding pain.

When you notice the urge to run away, bring your attention back to your body again. Don't judge yourself for wanting to avoid pain; everyone does that. Our minds are programmed to avoid pain and seek pleasure. The job of the mind is to protect us. Understand there is nothing wrong with distracting ourselves from our unpleasant feelings, but this is just one strategy.

There is a better way.

Instead of running away from pain, run towards it.

When we avoid our emotions, we tend to harden our bodies. Do the opposite. Relax your body and let go of any resistance you have. Surrender and allow your emotions to come up naturally. Remind yourself that loneliness is just an indicator we have disconnected from the love within. The emotion will be gone as soon as we allow the energy to move through our relaxed body. So instead of resisting unpleasant feelings, pay attention to the discomfort. There is no need to be protected in this circumstance. Be free of your emotions by expressing them and letting them go, rather than allowing them to remain stuck in your body.

This might sound rather counterintuitive, but before you can even let go of your emotions, you must first let them surface and acknowledge their existence. How can you let go of something when you don't even recognize you are holding it?

3. Allow your emotions to surface and let them go.

When you focus your attention on your body for a while, emotions other than loneliness, such as shame, fear, and anger, might start to surface. Allow these emotions to surface, feel the energy move through your body, and let them move out naturally. If this means you have to cry, allow yourself to cry. If your body starts to shake and tremble, allow it to do so. The body intuitively knows how to deal with emotion. So simply follow your body's wisdom and not resist it. Your body will guide you in taking the appropriate actions to help in the release of emotion. For example, when I feel a deep sense of longing for love and it feels like there's a hole in my chest area, I intuitively put my fist on my chest and it feels much better.

This process might feel frightening at first. It feels like you are losing control of your body. But know that experiencing emotions is not life-threatening. It will end eventually. Your body will know when to stop. Trusting your body is a form of surrender.

**Be careful not to let your mind get in
storytelling mode, because it will create
unnecessary suffering.**

There is a difference between the emotions aroused in
the body by triggering events, and the emotions generated
over and over again by the mind's ruminating about the
events. We need to understand the difference. Emotions
aroused in the body can be let go of very quickly when we
allow them to move through us when they first occur.
Feelings generated when the mind continues going over
and over the events that triggered our loneliness can be
never-ending.

So, for example, if you went to a social event and you
felt lonely, letting go of this emotion at the time it arises
will release the emotion from your body. But if you start to
analyze what happened, your underlying beliefs about
being unworthy and not fitting in anywhere can be
triggered. Your mind will begin to bring up events from the
past when you felt lonely, and it will start to tell a story. As
a result, more feelings of loneliness will be created. This can

go on for a long time, until you regain consciousness and snap out of the repetitive mind-loop stories created by your mind.

When a problem arises, our minds are programmed to find solutions and fix it, even if this means ruminating on the problem and finding someone to blame. If we don't see our emotions as problems, but simply as information that can help our growth, then letting go of emotion will be much easier.

4. Acknowledge your effort.

If this is the first time you are doing this practice, you might find it difficult. You might be tempted to give up halfway. Regardless of whether you fully release your emotions, or not, acknowledge your effort. Most of us are not trained to deal with our emotions, so it takes time to get better at it.

This practice helps us develop the quality of equanimity, which is the ability to welcome all of our feelings, while remaining calm and in balance, even if the situation is difficult. We want to cultivate the space within ourselves to allow all of our emotions to pass through. This will help us face all types of life situations with greater ease and peace. So the next time you feel lonely or any other troubling emotion, I invite you to tune in to the emotion, embrace it, and practice equanimity. Don't escape at this first sign of discomfort.

Even if you become unconscious and go into storytelling mode, know that you have just collected more data about your past conditioning, and you can work with it in the future. We aren't always aware of our loneliness, so be grateful for having this information.

In the next part of the book, we will explore the disconnection we feel as a result of the ego's incessant storytelling. Understanding the structure of the ego can help us understand why we keep feeling lonely.

PART 2

Understanding the Disconnection

Chapter 4

The Desire to Remain Separate

"The ego seeks to divide and separate. Spirit seeks to unify and heal."

— PEMA CHÖDRÖN

One night in July 2018, I had a dream. In the dream, I took a lift up to the sixtieth floor and it was pitch dark. I explored the place gingerly and when I turned around a corner, I was blinded by this white light. When I woke up, there was an image in my mind of my friend, Pat, and he was crying. I felt deep compassion for him. Then, I heard a voice tell me to contact Pat. Feeling puzzled, I asked, *Why do I have to contact Pat? What am I going to say to him?* The voice replied, *Be of service to him. Approach him. Show him what presence is.* I asked the voice how, but there was no answer.

The next day, I contacted Pat and asked him how he was doing. He said he had just come back from a holiday and felt fine. Feeling relieved that nothing bad had happened to Pat, I thought to myself, *Maybe the voice is wrong. But... maybe I could give him a copy of my book.* So I asked Pat if he would like a copy and he said, "Yes."

Previously, I had intended to give him a copy of my memoir, *The Emotional Gift*. He had been through similar experiences, so I thought he would find this book useful. But somehow I procrastinated. An unconscious part of me (the part I call *The Inner Child*) didn't want to do it. The last time I had given a book to a friend, there was no response. My inner child was so scared of being rejected again that I felt close-hearted and indifferent, rather than helpful and compassionate.

When the books arrived from the printer, I wanted to give Pat a copy. But for months, he was either too busy or traveling. I suggested we meet somewhere convenient for him. It would only take five minutes, but he just didn't seem to have the time. During this period, my inner child was getting impatient and resentful. Never had I been so angry. When I allowed my inner child to express itself through my body, I was literally stomping on the ground like a little boy throwing a tantrum for not getting what I wanted. It was interesting yet shocking to observe the strong emotions that were buried deep within me.

I could empathize with how insecure my inner child was feeling. When I first met Pat, he would reply to my messages and emails within a day or two. But now he disappears for days before sending a reply. Each time he goes missing, my inner child feels insecure and I wonder if I said or did something wrong. Once I wanted to write Pat a letter to help him understand his emotions better. However, once I made the decision, I noticed my body started trembling for no reason, especially my left hand. I asked my inner child what was wrong and it told me, *I beg you. Don't do this to me. I would not be able to take it if it doesn't go well.* When I finally gave the letter to him, I just wanted to disappear and bury myself. I felt like I had done something wrong.

Fortunately, I was aware of my inner child and I held space for the emotions to emerge, so I wasn't consumed by them. Everything was fine again after I soothed my inner child. Somehow, I also had this deep knowing that Pat would reply to me eventually, so I waited.

However, one night, my inner child lost it. For months, Pat hadn't contacted me to collect the book like he had promised. Instead, when he was available again, he went to social gatherings. I woke up in the middle of the night and my inner child began to cry, *He didn't have five minutes to meet me and pick up the book, but he had the time to socialize with others. They are all the same! They don't want to be my friend! No one wants to be my friend!* At that instant, I realized there was a lot more going on below the surface.

Although we want to be close with others, we maintain a distance so we won't be hurt.

After allowing my inner child to cry, I was able to calm down and process what had just happened. I realized my inner child was trying to affirm the negative beliefs, *I'm flawed. Other people don't like me.* and reenacting the same old abandonment stories I experienced in secondary school. Although I was angry with Pat for breaking his promises, I recognized my anger was an accumulation of all the bad experiences and unresolved emotional pain my inner child had been holding on to for years. Whenever I felt angry with Pat, I was reminded of all the people who had hurt me previously. Pat isn't the first person who broke a promise to me and was constantly unavailable. Yet, I kept attracting the same people into my life and experiencing the same feelings of abandonment, betrayal, and rejection. However, it wasn't until my friendship with Pat that I noticed this pattern.

I was given many opportunities to heal and forgive, but all I could see was how much others had hurt me. Instead of healing my pain, I've unknowingly collected more stories that add to my pain. After this incident, I realized that even if I continue to resent Pat and avoid talking to him, the Universe will bring the same type of people to me until I finally get the message. With this new revelation, I overcame my fear and simply gave Pat the book at a social event. Nothing really bad happened, like what my inner child had imagined, and Pat was happy to receive my gift.

Now, in hindsight, I realize my dream had nothing to do with Pat. It was more like a nudge from the Universe to remind me to be more compassionate and keep my heart open to others. The deepest part of my soul has the desire to love and connect with other people, but I can't do it while I'm still holding onto resentment and feeding the desire of my ego to remain separate.

The Game the Ego Plays

The ego thrives on separation and needs it to survive. The ego is developed as we learn what is "me" and what is "not me." Without this separation of "me" and "them," the ego cannot exist. It has to make everything personal so our identity can be maintained separately from everyone else, whether positive or negative.

The ego's desire to remain separate from others can be very subtle, but it's there all the time. When we compare ourselves with other people, when we judge ourselves or others as superior or inferior, and when we have conflicts with others, the ego is trying to create separation and keep us from being one with others.

Ironically, the ego also needs love, validation, and attention from other people in order to maintain an identity of desirability, superiority, and worthiness. Being validated by others gives us a sense of self-importance. We tell ourselves: *I am worthy of love. I am important to someone else. They want me.* These beliefs keep the ego alive. It can't afford to let us get too disconnected from others.

As much as we want to connect with others,
we also want to disconnect from others.

So...on one hand, we might tell ourselves we want to be close and intimate with others, but on the other hand, we also want to pull away. When we are in a close relationship with another person, the ego might cause us to bring up insignificant differences so we have a reason to argue with the people we love. It will point out our differences in terms of values, interests, beliefs, and personalities. What's worse is when we hold onto the position of being right and see others as being wrong. This creates conflicts that sometimes ruin our relationships.

The ego constantly fluctuates between these two conflicting desires. When we are too close to others, we are afraid of being consumed by them and we want to separate ourselves. But when we realize we are too distant from others, we want to reconnect with them and establish our significance. We switch from one extreme to the opposite extreme. This is the game the ego plays to capture our attention and maintain control of our consciousness.

Furthermore, the ego's incessant desire to connect with others reestablishes our deep-seated beliefs that we are separate from them. If we are not separate from others in the first place, why are we so desperate to reconnect with them? There will be a strong desire to grasp and hold onto another person only when our minds believe there is separation and we are incomplete without others.

From a spiritual perspective, there is no such disconnection. We are one with everyone and everything.

We might look and behave differently at the human-level, but deep down spiritually, we are all connected to the universal source of love. Only when we are overly immersed in our minds does our true nature become obscured and we can't feel the connection. All we can see is how separate we are. For years, I could only see how my friends hurt me. I kept repeating the same old story like a never-ending movie. Only when I became aware of the stories in my mind—and no longer identified with them—was I able to see how my ego has been using these false stories to build an identity separate from other people.

The Ego's Story Structure

As long as we are human, we will have an ego, and it will point out the differences between us and other people. The ego is not necessarily bad. It gives us a sense of identity. When it's healthy, it creates a separation that we humans need for survival, and it keeps us safe. But when it's unhealthy and we let the ego guide us instead of our soul, we become completely identified with the story the ego creates. We act from a place of fear instead of a place of love. We protect ourselves, even when protection is not needed.

The ego only understands love from

a survival perspective. It doesn't understand love from

a deeper, spiritual perspective.

From the ego's perspective, we need love from others to survive. We need to do things to make sure other people give us the love we need. But from a spiritual perspective, we are love and we don't need to do anything to make us feel love or feel worthy of love. If we just surrender to our true essence and don't block the love from flowing, love will come naturally. However, it's not easy to stay in the spiritual perspective for long, because the ego is a very good storyteller. No matter how many times we reconnect, we are easily drawn in by the stories and become disconnected from the spiritual dimension again. Sometimes, it can be more transformational to change the story itself than to keep letting go of our emotion, so the stories don't have a grip on us anymore.

Furthermore, the ego has a solid structure to keep things the way they are. This structure is not easy to tear down, because the ego is relentless at keeping this structure intact. Also, tearing down the structure all at once can bring about strong emotions that might overwhelm us, especially if we aren't inexperienced at dealing with our emotions. This structure has helped us survive childhood and protected us from the emotional pain that might be otherwise too difficult for us to deal with. We are so used to having this structure and so convinced of its validity that breaking it apart can turn our world upside down. With an awareness of the structure, we can erode it gradually in a gentle manner that doesn't trigger the ego to fight back.

The ego's structure can be divided into the following three main components:

1. **Events:** These serve as a constant stream of evidence to support our limiting beliefs and give us material for new stories to be written by the ego.
2. **Beliefs:** These help us form quick conclusions about ourselves and others, so opposing opinions and evidence will be excluded from our awareness the next time they occur.
3. **Habits:** These help make our beliefs stronger by repeating actions and behaviors that support our beliefs.

These three components strengthen and reinforce each other. Without any one of these components, the structure will be significantly weaker, and the stories that the ego tells will be less appealing. In the next three chapters, we will discuss each component in depth. But for now, here's a simple example from the opening story of this chapter to briefly illustrate the three components.

Events

One of the previous events that caused me to feel disconnected from other people was when I felt abandoned by my friend. James was my secondary school classmate, and we used to be very good friends. However, he started distancing himself from me when another one of his friends said James and I were too close and that we seemed like "a couple." Ironically, instead of telling the naysayer off, James became better friends with him and he and I grew apart. I felt rather disappointed and betrayed by James, especially because I didn't have many friends at that time. But when I left school and didn't see them again, I forgot about this incident. I was reminded of James only when I met Pat for the first time because they looked alike.

The incident with Pat made me realize that I hadn't forgiven James for what he had done, and I hadn't fully processed my hurt feelings. In fact, it made me afraid of being seen as too close to another person. Subconsciously, I was afraid that if I got too close to Pat or gave him the book in front of everyone, I would attract the same negative attention and jealousy from his other friends, and it would ruin our friendship. So I preferred to give my book to Pat in private. However, when Pat didn't contact me to collect the book, I was forced to give it to him in public, which greatly upset my inner child. This is why it brought out the anger, fear, and anxiety of my inner child.

Beliefs

One belief I didn't even know I had (until my inner child cried out that night) is that no one wants to be my friend, and I will eventually be abandoned. Even though after the incident with James I made a lot of friends, I didn't consider any of these friendships to be close, and I wouldn't contact any of them if I needed help. I always changed my core group of friends as I progressed through different stages in my life. Some of these friends I met in schools; some I met at work or in common interest groups. But none of them lasted. Once I reached each stage of my life and moved on, we would gradually stop contacting each other. I thought it was normal for friends to come and go.

Now I realize I never truly believed anyone could be interested in being my friend, so I seldom took the initiative or made an effort to stay in contact. I was afraid of being rejected and being disappointed when they turned down my invitations. I also kept a safe distance from potential friends so there would be no possibility of getting hurt. When you don't trust that other people are interested in being your friend, you will find it difficult to be close and intimate with anyone, because deep down inside you feel insecure about yourself and your relationships. You don't want to be too invested in any relationship, because you expect the other person to abandon you at some point. By maintaining a distance with others, you won't feel so hurt when they leave you.

Habits

Holding this subconscious belief caused me to develop the habit of making friends with people who were often busy and unavailable. There are many others who are less busy and have more time for me. But if people approach me too frequently or with too much eagerness, I'm not interested in being friends with them. Somehow, I'm more drawn to people who have no time for me or who are emotionally distant. By being friends with these types of people, I am more likely to get rejected and not get the connection I desire. Unavailable people help me recreate the same feelings of abandonment and betrayal that I once felt in school. They provide new evidence to strengthen my negative beliefs about myself.

Due to my belief that I will be eventually abandoned, I have also developed the habit of overthinking relationships. When my friends pull away from me or don't reply to my messages, I start to worry whether I did or said something wrong, even though their behavior might have nothing to do with me. I have developed hypervigilance to make sure I am not abandoned again, but this habit of seeking traces of abandonment makes me feel unnecessarily anxious and insecure.

I also have a habit of backing off and withdrawing if I sense that one of my friends is keen to connect with another one of my friends. I allow them to be closer to each other and not get in their way. Partly, this evokes the same emotional pain of being replaced and no longer needed when my friend, James, chose someone else over me. But more importantly, doing this makes me feel envious of them and reestablishes that I will never have close friendships like other people do.

Chapter 5

The Events That Wound Us

"Your task is not to seek for love, but merely to seek and find all the barriers within yourself that you have built against it."

— RUMI

I never realized how abandoned I felt as a kid. Abandonment is not even a word I would use to describe my childhood, because my parents were always physically there with me. They never left my siblings and me for a long period of time for work or any other reason. It wasn't until after the incident with Pat that I started recognizing the deep sense of abandonment my inner child carried. Over the next few months, I discovered more events that suggested I might have felt emotionally abandoned or neglected as a kid.

One of my major discoveries occurred in April 2019,

when I attended an online masterclass created by Mindvalley and Marisa Peer. During the class, Marisa conducted a hypnotherapy session with all of the participants. We went back into our past and pulled out three events that caused us to feel rejected.

The first scene that came to mind was when I was around ten years old. My mom was busy doing housework and didn't have the time to help me revise my spelling test. Her refusal to help made me feel unimportant. The second scene was when I was an infant. I was longing for attention from my parents, but they seemed more interested in playing with my elder brother than attending to me. This made me feel that I'm not worthy of their attention. The last scene was when I was a fetus inside my mom's womb. I felt rejected because she wanted a girl instead of a boy. I'm not sure if my mind made up the second two events because I have no conscious memory of anything before the age of five, but they do *feel* true. I also experienced similar events when I was much older.

A week after the class, the rain was pouring heavily outside, and I woke up in the middle of the night with the image of my two-year-old self foremost in my mind. I remembered wanting to be hugged and carried by my parents, but they neglected me. I waited for a long time, but no one came to pick me up. I felt very sad and abandoned, and in the end, I gave up. After this realization, I finally understood why I felt so uncomfortable when I saw my friend leave her crying baby boy to deal with his emotions on his own. I was that same little child who didn't get picked up and soothed.

You might not remember everything from your past, but recent events can give you a clue about how you might have felt as a child.

Four months later, I attended my auntie's sixtieth birthday celebration with my family. At the end of the dinner, my aunt's church friends hugged my mom, and she looked so happy and keen to hug them back. I blurted out to my elder brother, "Mom never hugs me like that." After we went back home, my brother told my mom that I wanted her to hug me, too. So I stood up with my arms wide open, but my mom remained motionless. She looked uncomfortable, as though she didn't want to hug me. I stood there feeling the same disappointment and abandonment I felt as a child. It was only when my brother urged my mom to reciprocate that she stood up and gave me a half-hearted side hug and a consolation pat on the back.

Now, I understand why it's so difficult for me to approach others and show them affection. When you feel rejected by your parents as a child, it will be difficult for you to be affectionate when you become an adult. You come to believe that you are unlovable and people will reject your love. So you learn to be aloof and passive, waiting for someone to initiate contact, which only makes others think that you are unapproachable or uninterested.

The Purpose of Revisiting Past Events

As mentioned in my previous book, *Parent Yourself Again*, when we reflect on our past, we are not trying to blame our parents for what they have done (or not done) or get them to change. They also had unpleasant experiences in childhood, and they did the best they could with their level of awareness. We might not have received the unconditional love and affection we deserved as a child, but this shouldn't be our excuse to remain a victim. We have to be responsible for our growth, actions, and behaviors.

When we revisit our childhood, we want to see if there are any overlooked emotions we have not processed completely. Certain emotions, such as grief and helplessness, are too overwhelming to cope with when we are children, and we might have suppressed them or developed beliefs and habits to work around them. In my case, I didn't process my fear of abandonment and rejection. I continued to let it manifest repeatedly in my adult relationships. Also, when we were children, we didn't have the language we needed to describe to our parents how we felt. If we didn't have sensitive or empathetic parents — who were willing to help us move through these emotions — it's highly likely our unprocessed emotions are still stuck in our bodies.

Uncovering past events is a good way to learn whether we have let go of our emotions related to past events. If we still tear up or get triggered when we talk about the past, it usually means we still have a lot of emotions buried within us. If we are at peace with the events of our lives, we will be able to share what we experienced without much difficulty or reactivity.

The purpose of examining past events is also to see how we can come to perceive those events differently. As Marisa Peer says in her masterclass:

"Events don't affect you.

It's the meaning you attach to them that does."

The events we have experienced are factual, but our interpretation of them is subjective and can be changed. Revisiting past events gives us a chance to reinterpret those events through a different lens, especially the meanings we created in childhood. As children, we depend on our parents for love, so it feels scary when our parents don't give us attention and love. But now, as adults, even when other people reject us or deny us their attention, we won't die because of it. Being ignored doesn't threaten our survival. We have developed better coping skills. We are no longer helpless children. If we understand that our past perceptions were those of a helpless child, and we can change our perceptions, we can change how we respond to similar events when we are adults.

Finally, being aware of past events can also help us be more mindful. It's easier to catch the ego telling the same old blame stories from the past when we know what they are. Then we can choose to let go of the old stories and not let them color our perception of current events.

How to Uncover Past Events

Some of the events that have wounded us are not so obvious, because we experienced them when we were very young and we might have repressed the bad memories. To access memories that are deeply buried in your subconscious, techniques such as hypnosis can help.

There is no need to dig up all the events that have wounded you. They will surface on their own when it's time for them to be healed.

Even though the earliest event you remember might be the origin of your disconnection, and releasing it can free you from many limiting beliefs and suffering, the story the ego tells is built and strengthened by multiple events, not just a single event. So letting go of the little stories and changing our perspectives on them can also help chip away at the structure the ego has in place. It's better to work on events you remember first, and allow the others to surface in their own time. It's less overwhelming that way.

If you don't recall any past troubling events, pay attention to the current events that make you feel lonely. The newer events are usually reenactments of earlier events. As mentioned before, your current reaction will give you clues as to how you might have felt in the past, especially if the people you are interacting with now were also present in your childhood.

Furthermore, current events are usually what trigger the ego to retell the story. The ego pulls events from the past to interpret current events, which adds to the whole narrative the ego is building. You might not be consciously thinking about past events, but when your ego brings you back to the past, it's an opportunity for you to discover the wounds you are still holding onto. For example, the incident I had with Pat is between Pat and I. But when my mind started to regurgitate the mental content from the past to justify my experience with Pat, I became aware that I hadn't fully let go of these past events. Other examples could be when you hear a song or see a memento that reminds you of the past. They can also reveal past events that are still hurting you in the present.

When you feel lonely, ask yourself: *What just happened that triggered my feeling of loneliness? Are there any particular things that people say or do that cause me to feel lonely? Is being in a specific scenario or environment causing my feelings of disconnection?*

Pay attention to the story you tell yourself concerning

the events. Again, your interpretation is more important than the events themselves.

You also want to look for patterns. Have you been in similar situations before? Did similar events happen in the past that made you feel lonely? Is your loneliness usually triggered when you are alone, or does it occur when you are with other people? Do you often feel lonely when people don't understand you or when they don't pay attention to you? You can also ask yourself: *What were my unmet needs in childhood? Did I wish my parents would hug me more, be more affectionate, be more interested in me, and spend more time with me? Is the current event causing my loneliness lonely a reflection of my unmet needs in childhood?* Asking these questions will get you started and help you uncover the major events in the past that are still causing you to feel lonely.

Three Types of Events That Cause Loneliness

There are many events from childhood that can make you feel disconnected in adulthood. Some are obvious, but others aren't as impactful, so we might not see the link between these events and our perpetual sense of disconnection.

To give you some ideas about what these events might

be, I've broken them into three main categories:

- Events when other people moved away from you,
- Events when you moved away from others, and
- Events related to a wall between you and others.

For each category, I'll start with events we experience in adulthood, and their relation to the events we experienced in childhood.

When Other People Move Away From You

Of the three categories, this is probably the easiest one to identify. When we realize other people are moving away from us, our typical interpretation is that they don't love us; they don't want to be around us; there's something we do or say that is causing them to leave us; or they have some other reason. These events cause us to feel abandoned, excluded, and unwanted.

Examples of events in this category experienced in adulthood include: when your partner breaks up with you; losing your partner due to death; when your friends distance themselves; when your best friend migrates to another country; when someone rejects or ignores your messages; or for some other reason. Loneliness might not be the first emotion we feel when such events occur. Instead, these events might trigger insecurity and separation anxiety, at first, and we start to cling to the other person or memories of the lost relationship.

During adolescence, it's also common to be excluded and rejected by our peers. Some of us have issues relating to our peers in school. Due to our shyness or personality, we might find it difficult to join or form cliques. If we are too different from our peers, we might find ourselves being the outcast. This is the age when we try to find our place socially, so feeling accepted and included by peers is important.

However, it is also an age when we are most likely to be self-absorbed. Our peers might say or do things without much consideration for how other people feel, and we are easily wounded by their actions and words. Most of the time, we don't know why our peers exclude us, and we end up forming various negative beliefs about ourselves to justify the exclusion. Even though we might have become better at connecting with other people, as adults these beliefs are still deeply entrenched in our minds.

Childhood loss and abandonment can also be the foundation on which the ego builds its story. Events such as the divorce of our parents, the loss of our parents, or even the loss of our siblings can lead to fear of abandonment. When your main caretakers are frequently absent from your life, or they are not emotionally present even when they are physically present, you can also feel abandoned; for example, when one or both of your parents is chronically sick; your parents are struggling with addictions; or your parents are always gone because they are working.

If your loneliness is a result of feeling abandoned by others, take a look at your childhood.

Adults actually cannot be abandoned by other people; only children can. Unlike children, most adults can meet their own physical and emotional needs. When someone ends a relationship with us or distances themselves, it's not abandonment because we can survive on our own. The other person is not responsible for our needs. They are free to do whatever they want. Yes, we might feel sad and disappointed over the loss of the relationship. But if we feel abandoned, anxious, and resentful towards them for leaving us or being unavailable—as though they are supposed to meet our needs—it usually points to something bigger that we experienced in childhood.

Sometimes, it's not easy to see our abandonment in childhood. In my case, I didn't experience physical abandonment, but rather emotional abandonment. My parents gave me shelter and food, and provided me with all my physical needs. But they neglected to give me enough praise, affection, attention, and acknowledgment.

As children grow older, parents have to let their children learn to be independent and grow by themselves. But this separation needs to be done properly and gradually. If it occurs before the child is ready for separation and is able to handle his or her emotions, the child can become wounded and carry the wound into adulthood.

When You Move Away From Others

Loneliness can also happen when we move away from others. We might isolate ourselves as a means to protect ourselves from being hurt or judged. This disconnection is usually created by fear.

Adults who have a fear of intimacy might long for closeness, but they end up sabotaging their relationships and push other people away when things get too close for comfort. We withdraw because the closer other people get to us, the more we worry they will discover the flaws we believe we have and want to hide. When people know too much about us, we put ourselves at risk of being abandoned or rejected. Some of us even go to the extreme and give up on dating and love relationships altogether in order to prevent our getting hurt. We tell ourselves we don't need anyone else. But deep down inside, we suffer an inability to trust anyone and we fear being vulnerable.

Events that cause us to feel disappointed with others, or ourselves, can also cause us to withdraw and increase our feeling of loneliness. For example, when our friends don't live up to our expectations or they do something that betrays our trust, we might not want to interact with them anymore. Sometimes, we isolate ourselves because we think we have done something wrong, and we feel like our friends are not going to perceive us in the same, positive light anymore. There are also some events that make us feel like we are not good enough. For example, we lose our job or we are down with a chronic illness, and we believe that others will look down on us and so we withdraw from them.

The main sources of our constant feelings of separation

are the childhood events

that undermine our trust in others.

Sometimes, our mistrust of people can be traced to childhood experiences of abandonment, abuse, or neglect. Especially if we were abused as children, our ability to trust others will be significantly reduced. As children, if we can't trust our parents or caretakers to take care and protect us, then who can we trust? Not only do we experience a lot of anger towards the abuser, but we also learn early in life to guard ourselves against people and keep a safe distance from others, even those we want to be close to us.

Our insecurity and mistrust block us from receiving love from others and forming intimate relationships, causing us to misread people who are safe. Instead, we gravitate towards people who are abusive because they affirm our belief that others will hurt us. When we get into abusive relationships, it only makes it harder for us to trust others.

When There's a Wall Between You and Others

Sometimes, we feel lonely even when no one is moving

away from us. We can be surrounded by many people we love and we still don't feel any connection with them. It feels like there's a wall between other people and us. We don't resonate with them. The things they are interested in are not what we are interested in, and we often don't just feel lonely, we feel misunderstood and not accepted.

A wall between two people usually occurs when either or both parties cannot understand each other completely. It might be a difference in terms of our personality, preferences, values, opinions, experiences, background, or some other difference. Sometimes, no matter how much we try to relate and communicate with another person, they just don't get us. Some people are so fixated on their mental positions that they are not able to see other perspectives or accept that other people are different. It can be frustrating to share our deepest thoughts and feelings with someone and constantly be unacknowledged. So we stop sharing and only communicate on a superficial level.

People who grow up with disorders such as autism and Asperger's syndrome will naturally have difficulties getting others to understand them. But people who grow up with indifferent or neglectful parents will also likely experience disconnection with other people when they become adults.

If you often feel lonely and misunderstood,
you most likely didn't receive enough mirroring
as a kid.

"Mirroring" means that when a baby coos or tries to communicate in gibberish, the parents respond by doing the same, copying the baby's body language and matching the tone of the baby. Mirroring helps build connections between the parents and the child. It shows the children that their parents understand their emotional state and are attuned to them.

However, if you have parents who aren't sensitive enough to notice what you are feeling, or they are emotionally blocked, they won't be able to mirror your emotions back to you. Also, if you have parents who want you to be like them and force their opinions on you, instead of acknowledging how you feel and your desires, you will not be able to develop a unique sense of self and identity. Rather than feeling connected with your parents, you will be disconnected not just with your parents, but also with yourself.

Being emotionally neglected and ignored as a child, you are likely to feel insignificant, unimportant, unheard, misunderstood, and lonely—even when you become an adult. There will always be a desire and longing for other people to understand, see, and hear you. But you often end up feeling like something is missing from your relationships. There is an invisible wall between you and others that was formed way back in childhood when your emotional needs were not met. Your current disconnection with others is just a reflection of your disconnection with your parents.

Chapter 6

The Beliefs That Keep Us Stuck

"You cannot be lonely if you like the person you're alone with."

— WAYNE DYER

Behind every story of loneliness, there is an overarching theme. For the longest time, the theme of my story was *nobody likes me.*

It all started on the first day of secondary school. During assembly, my mom went to the boy in front of me and asked him to be my friend. At the time, I felt embarrassed, and I thought to myself: *I'm 13 years old. I know how to make friends, mom!* But at the same time, I felt as though there was something wrong with me if I needed my mom to help me fit in.

My mom had all the right reasons for her behavior.

The night before the first day of school, she was taken aback when I cried in front of her. I didn't cry when I started kindergarten or primary school, and I don't know what came over me this time. Having never been to a camp or away from home before, I was probably terrified by the three-day bonding camp all the new students had to participate in before the start of the term. The new environment was scary, but I was probably more scared of living with strangers.

After the camp, I felt left out. Many of my classmates were from the same primary school, so they already knew each other. Even though I also knew someone from my previous school, we weren't that close and I felt alone when I saw him form a clique quickly without me. I managed to make two friends who also hadn't known anyone previously. One of them was James, but you know what happened to our friendship in the end. Making friends became the biggest issue for my four years in secondary school, especially the first year.

My first form teacher paired us up according to our names, and we had to do most of our activities with our partner. It would have been great if we had gotten along, but we didn't. We are supposed to line up with each other when we move from venue to venue. But sometimes my partner would disappear into the back of the line and leave me alone in front leading the class to the next venue. Not only did my partner not want to pair up with me, he often forced another student to exchange places with him. Whenever they quarreled, it made me feel so unwanted and I would wonder:

What's wrong with me?

Why doesn't anyone want to pair up with me?

Gradually, after several similar unhappy experiences in school, I *concluded* that no one liked me and no one was interested in being my friend. I thought I was too boring for other people. Whenever our class had an excursion, I would be one of the first to get on the bus. I didn't want to sit next to another student and force the student to have a conversation with me. I always let others "choose" whether they wanted to sit with me, or not.

Feeling lonely and having no one to share with, I would write my feelings down on small pieces of paper and bury them in the ground. I missed my primary school friends, but I didn't have their contact numbers. There weren't any mobile phones or social media at that time, and

I thought they had already moved on and found new friends, too. I also didn't share my difficulties with my family because I didn't want them to worry about me. I told my dad that I wanted to change schools, but my request was rejected without further inquiry from him. So for the next four years, I just pretended I was doing fine in school, while in reality, I couldn't wait to graduate and get away.

Thankfully, after my secondary school days, I had more agreeable classmates and friends. But even though they were nice to me, I still had the belief that no one liked me. If you have read my book, *Empty Your Cup*, you know this lasted until my first job, when I broke down in the office toilet cubicle and decided to do something about my low self-esteem. Ever since I let go of my limiting beliefs, the critical narrative in my head has subsided tremendously.

How Our Beliefs Keep Us Stuck in Loneliness

If our interpretations of past events are like building blocks or bricks, then our belief system is like the glue or cement that holds the ego's story together. Our perception of a singular event can hurt us badly. But it's the same perception of multiple events that form beliefs and keep us locked in a perpetual loop of loneliness. If you keep telling yourself the same thing, your mind will soon believe it's true, regardless of whether it is, or not.

Once a belief is formed and a conclusion has been reached, the mind starts to find more proof to support the belief and make it stronger. The mind ignores any evidence that is contrary to the belief. More often than not, our minds distort and exaggerate reality to fit our existing belief. The mind is a very efficient system. It doesn't waste any effort and time in re-examining similar events once a conclusion has been made. Instead, it directs its attention to new scenarios in which no conclusion has been reached. Our interpretation of events becomes automatic. They are not based on each situation, as it is. The problem with this is that most of our beliefs were formed when we were young and impressionable, and misinterpretation was most likely to occur. So many of us still carry childhood beliefs that do not serve us in our adult lives.

Furthermore, your beliefs dictate your actions, which further strengthen your beliefs. If you believed people don't want to be with you, wouldn't you withdraw and keep your distance from them? How do you approach someone and connect with them deeply when you feel they don't like you? Even if they are friendly, you will doubt their sincerity and intention.

Our beliefs are not permanent.

They are just our habitual way of thinking.

Our beliefs are made in our minds, and anything that is created by the mind can be recreated. We can change our beliefs or choose new ways of thinking. However, most of us don't do this because we are so convinced by the ego's story that we cannot see any other perspective. We would rather protect our beliefs than challenge them.

Moreover, beliefs are not always easy to identify. Many thoughts are running through our minds each day, and most of them are automatic. Without enough awareness, we might not be conscious of the things we tell ourselves. Also, our beliefs don't always come in the form of words. They can also be in the form of images; sometimes, we just have a feeling that something is true for us. For example, you might intellectually know that your loved ones care deeply for you, but you still feel doubtful, unloved, and lonely.

Our beliefs generate thoughts that evoke certain feelings in us. To stop ourselves from being stuck in loneliness, we have to identify these beliefs and change our habitual way of thinking.

Identifying Your Beliefs Relating to Loneliness

My fourth book, *The Disbelief Habit*, is about changing the habit of self-criticism. There is a chapter in that book focusing on beliefs affecting self-esteem. Low self-esteem and negative self-perception can make us feel lonely, too. However, here I have focused only on the specific beliefs that evoke feelings of loneliness. These beliefs usually have to do with how we perceive our relationships and how we think others perceive us.

There are a couple of ways to find out your hidden beliefs. First, whenever you feel lonely, ask yourself:

What am I thinking right now that prevents me from feeling the love and connection I desire?

Love flows naturally when there are zero psychological barriers. If you don't feel love, there must be something you believe that is causing this disconnection. It could be a belief about yourself or someone else. It could be a belief that prevents you from receiving or giving love. You might also have a belief about a condition you think you need to satisfy before you will be worthy of love.

We want to be more mindful and skeptical of our thoughts. Most of our thoughts are automatically churned out by our minds and based on our outdated belief system. Thus, they tend to be similar. Once you identify a pattern, you will know the beliefs that are constantly generating your feeling of loneliness.

Alternatively, below are some common beliefs relating to loneliness. Read them aloud and pause to check the reaction in your body. If your body reacts to any of these beliefs strongly, or they evoke a feeling of loneliness or sadness, it means you probably have this belief.

No One Cares About Me

Other similar beliefs: No one likes me; no one loves me; no one supports what I do; no one wants to be around me; no one notices me.

A common belief that evokes loneliness is: *No one cares about me.* You can replace the words "cares about" with other words such as "likes," "loves," "listens to," "supports," "wants," or "notices," and you will get the same feeling of isolation. This belief evokes a lot of pain because it makes us feel invisible, unwanted, and unimportant. It tells us that we don't matter to other people, especially those people we care about and desire love from.

As mentioned in my book, *The Disbelief Habit*, the words "no one" sound dramatic but they cannot be validated. You can't know for sure that no one loves you unless you check in with everyone, and since there's no way to verify it with every person living on the planet, this statement cannot be proven. Furthermore, this statement can't be true unless you don't love yourself.

I understand there are moments in life when we feel as though no one cares about us, times when the core people in our lives are not as supportive or loving as we want them to be. But we have forgotten that we are enough and complete on our own. We can't depend on others all the time, but we can always be there for ourselves. Not being there for yourself when you need it is a form of self-abandonment. It means you don't value yourself enough and you are not taking full responsibility for your needs.

This belief usually stems from low-self esteem or from our expectations of others.

We think other people don't care about us because we

are unworthy of their attention. There's something we are ashamed of about ourselves that makes it difficult for us to believe people will like us. To delve deeper into your beliefs and understand what aspects of yourself you have issues with, complete this sentence: *No one likes me because....*

I used to think no one wanted to talk to me because I was too quiet and boring. So I withdrew, and this made me feel even lonelier. But now I understand that I should not use the amount of social interaction I have to determine my likability. I am quiet, but this doesn't mean other people don't enjoy being around me. Some people admire my quiet presence, while others just don't know how to approach me and start a conversation because they are also afraid of rejection.

Other times, this type of belief can be a result of our unmet expectations of others. Here are some examples of such expectations:

- If they care about me, they will remember my birthday and return my texts.
- If they love me, they won't criticize me. They will support me.
- If they enjoy hanging out with me, they will take

the initiative to contact me and spend more time with me.

- If they are truly interested in me, they will wait for me to finish talking and not interrupt me.
- If we are truly close, they will trust me with their problems.

Having these kinds of expectations prevents us from forming deep relationships with others. Everyone has their preferences. Some people are passive and prefer more time alone, so they would rather their friends contact them first. Others are very private. They don't wish to share something personal even with their closest friends. Some are absent-minded and might forget your birthday or neglect to return your texts, but it doesn't mean they don't care about you. When we assume other people have the same preferences and expectations as we do—and we judge them for not meeting these expectations—it creates misunderstandings and leaves us feeling disappointed all the time.

I'll Always Be Alone

Other similar beliefs: I'll never find that special someone; I'm destined to be single; I'll never get married; I'm not going to experience love; I'm going to be alone forever.

This belief has to do with not getting the romantic relationship you want. The words "no one," "always," and "never" are words that our minds often use to exaggerate how bad our situation is. Being alone now doesn't mean we will be alone forever. It just means we are alone at this moment.

> **This belief brings a sense of hopelessness about the future. When we have such beliefs, it's easy to fall into self-pity mode.**

You want love but you don't believe you deserve it. You think your flaws prevent you from forming loving relationships. This belief might also be a result of a major breakup or losing someone special and you can't cope with it. You believe you will never experience the same kind of love again, or that there are people available but they are not the people you want to date or be close to. Some of us are attracted to unavailable people. We long for love we can never have in an effort to reenact our childhood experiences of not getting the love we desired from our parents. So we keep finding people who don't reciprocate our love to reaffirm that we are not good enough and we are destined to be single forever. Unless we process the grief we carry from childhood and allow ourselves to have love in the present, we will keep longing for the love that is missing — instead of experiencing the love that is currently available.

Behind these beliefs, there is also a belief suggesting that being alone or single is bad. As mentioned in Chapter 1, this is often the result of our social conditioning. We believe we need someone else in our lives in order to feel complete. But the truth is no one can complete us because we are already complete on our own. Others can only remind us of the wholeness we already are. Buying into these beliefs only trains us to focus on the love outside of us — instead of the love that is within us.

They Are Happier Without Me

Other similar beliefs: They are better off without me; they don't need me; I don't matter to them; they should stay away from me; they are more interested in each other than what I have to share.

We formed this belief when we experienced some kind of social exclusion and rejection in the past. This belief has to do with what you think other people prefer to have in a friend or a family member. You believe you lack these qualities, or other people have more of such qualities than you, and therefore you are not getting the love and attention other people are getting. For example, you might believe that others prefer friends who are more extroverted, friendly, funny, optimistic, and charming, and since you don't possess these traits, you are less desirable.

We think we know what other people want and what's best, so we decide for them, instead of allowing them to make their own choices.

When we have such beliefs, we tend to withdraw and isolate ourselves without giving others a chance to get to know us better. In a way, we've made a decision on their behalf based on what we have seen, and we've concluded they do not want to interact with us.

Even though some people find it easier to connect, this doesn't mean they are not interested in connecting with us. Yes, they might have their preferences of who they like to talk to, but most of us want variety in our lives. We want different types of friends—friends we can have deep conversations with; friends who share the same interests as us; and friends we hang out with regularly. Give them the power to choose who they want to interact with instead of deciding for them and holding back your desire to connect.

Apart from loneliness, you might also want to check whether there are underlying emotions. How do you conclude that people are happier without you? Is your belief shame-based or envy-based? Examples of shame-based beliefs might be you are sick or depressed and you don't wish to be a burden on other people. You might have been abused in the past and you feel unworthy. If your belief is envy-based, then it's probably because you doubt your desirability and feel insecure or threatened about your position in other people's hearts. You feel that other people are getting along better with each other than with you.

Even though this belief seems to focus on others, it points to a core issue many of us have deep down inside: we don't believe we are lovable enough. We believe we will always be rejected by others, so we give up on relationships whenever there is the slightest hint of rejection. When we feel unlovable, we tend to be passive and wait for other people to take an interest in us or welcome us into a group, instead of being proactive in building relationships. We want others to validate that we are lovable before we invest in a relationship.

However, this belief, like most other beliefs, is usually self-fulfilling. When you withdraw, other people might think you are not interested in them, so they leave you alone. Hence, you receive more evidence to support your belief that others are happier without you.

I Don't Fit in Anywhere

Other similar beliefs: I am too different from others; there's no one else like me; they don't understand what I'm going through; I can't connect with others on a deeper level; I can't relate to the people around me.

This belief has to do with our negative perception of being different. Instead of appreciating our uniqueness, we think people don't like us, or we have difficulty fitting in because we are too different from others.

To connect with others, we are required to look for similarities. But some of us are programmed to look for differences.

Everyone is different. No two humans are the same. If we were to focus on our differences, we definitely can find many. Being different isn't bad, but if we just focus on how different we are from others, it does not help us connect with them. Social connection is about finding something you have in common with other people.

However, some of us didn't receive enough mirroring during childhood. Our early interactions with our parents were based on contrasts, not similarities. We are led to believe we need to set ourselves apart and be special, so our parents will notice us. Trying to find similarities with others just reminds us of the pain we felt as children when our parents failed to connect with us.

Furthermore, justifying the idea that our parents don't love us — by thinking they can't relate to us because of our differences — helps minimize the deeper pain of feeling unloved. This is more bearable for a child. At least there is something we can work on, which is to get our parents to understand our unique identity. We believe that when our parents finally understand us, we will feel the love that we long for, and so we carry the same belief into adulthood. What we don't realize is that when we accentuate how different we are from others, we make it more difficult for others to connect with us. Our constant desire to get other people to understand us and accept our differences pushes them away, instead of drawing them to us. People either see us as self-centered and individualistic, or they can't fully comprehend us the way we want them to. This eventually leads us to more loneliness.

Finally, the mind likes to play the game of fitting in. Our minds are constantly evaluating whether we belong to a group, or not. In the past, it was important to belong to a tribe, because if we didn't we would be left to fend for ourselves in dangerous environments, where we could become food for predators. But nowadays, we don't face such dangers, and we are all evolving at various speeds. We can be "in" a group this moment and "out" of it the next moment. When there is a common purpose, we come together and when there is no longer a purpose to stick around, we go our separate ways. It's not always beneficial to stay in the same group. From the mental perspective, we either fit in or we stand out. There is nothing in-between. However, true belonging and significance lie in the formless when we are deeply connected with our spirit and the cosmos. It's not about fitting in to feel accepted or standing out to get noticed.

Chapter 7

The Habits That Sustain Our Loneliness

"Every action you take is a vote for the type of person you wish to become."

— JAMES CLEAR, ATOMIC HABITS

One day in 2018, I was on the bus and I was feeling bored, so I started mindlessly browsing the Facebook app on my mobile phone. When I saw a photo of my friends having dinner together, my first thought was: *Why wasn't I invited?*

Having practiced mindfulness for a couple of years, I knew I had to stay present and not let what I saw turn into a victim story. But it was too late; the "poison" had already spread into my body. Even though I switched off the app immediately and tried not to think about it, I felt a cold pang surging through me. For the next two days, I was knocked nearly unconscious. I kept thinking: *What's wrong with me? Why wasn't I invited?* The feeling of not being good enough started creeping back again, and I blamed my friends for abandoning me. I was brought back to the time when I had been left out by my peers.

In secondary one, I was the class secretary. But when I came back from recess one day, I realized that the class committee was having a meeting without me. Being the only person not invited for the meeting, I dared not enter the classroom. I thought to myself, *What if they don't want me in the meeting? I would feel so embarrassed if I barged in abruptly?* So I just stood outside of the classroom, hid in a corner, and watched them chatting happily through the gap between the window panes. When recess was over, no one said anything to me about the meeting. Ever since then, this image of me standing outside the classroom has been stuck in my head.

Even now as an adult, when I talk to others in a group, sometimes an invisible wall appears between us. It's as though we are separated by a classroom. I feel excluded and left out, especially if they are laughing among themselves and I'm not involved in the conversation. I slowly drift away, become disengaged, and participate less in the conversation. Over time, this has become a habit. The more people in a group, the less engaged I become and the more I feel unnecessary.

Sometimes, awareness is not enough.
Some of your habits have such strong momentum that
they will pull you in a direction you don't want to go.

I knew that dwelling on the Facebook photo would send me into self-pity mode. But my body still carried so much emotional pain from the past that I was dragged out of stillness. I couldn't help but think I had been abandoned by my friends. I wasn't present and grounded enough at that time, and I was unable to stop the momentum in my mind and body. My mind was so used to telling the same old story, and my body was so used to reacting to it, that merely being aware of the story was not enough to prevent me from being brought back to the past. It took two days to snap out of it, and for months afterward, I kept returning to the space of loneliness and abandonment, from time to time, until I took action and changed some of my habits.

Belief, in itself, is a thinking habit. We are in the habit of thinking the same thoughts repeatedly. We have already touched on some basic beliefs in the previous chapter.

Here, the focus is on behavioral habits — the habitual actions we take that create our loneliness.

The Habit of Using Technology Mindlessly

Some people think that developments in technology, such as social media, make us more connected; others think social media makes us feel more disconnected. The truth is technology is neutral. Social media is just a medium for us to communicate with each other despite the physical distance between us.

However, technology can magnify the existing problems of the human race and individuals. If you are someone who gets lonely or envious of others easily, technology will amplify these feelings. If you have past issues that you haven't dealt with, there are now more trigger points when you use social media. If you have a fear of missing out, then you can't help but launch your social media apps to see what other people are doing. And when you see other people do things without you, feelings of exclusion will arise, even if they are involved in something you are not interested in. Eckhart Tolle, the spiritual teacher, said it best: technology is an extension and amplification of the human mind. If we know how to use our minds, we will be able to use technology effectively.

Be mindful of how you use technology, because technology can give you too much information, or false and incomplete information.

In my case, I wouldn't have known my friends had dinner without me if it wasn't for technology. I don't need to know that I wasn't invited, but technology gave me access to such information. Technology can also lead us to misinterpret the behavior of others. For example, some messenger apps, such as Whatsapp, show the user whether the messages they sent have been received and read by the recipients. The app also shows you if your friends are online and whether they are typing a message to you. Seeing your message read but not replied to can be upsetting and create anxiety if you feel insecure about your relationships.

Furthermore, not all the information you see online is accurate. Sometimes, people who are depressed and lonely post happy photos of themselves online. The pretense is brought to another level on social media. Not only do people have to pretend they are happy in front of others, they now have to show they are happy online, too. Seeing happy photos of other people might make you feel worse about yourself. You might start to wonder: *Why is everyone but me getting what they want? Why do they have so many friends and I don't? Why are they close to their family but I'm not?* When we consume information online, we have to be mindful that the information might be incomplete or incorrect. Often, people would rather share their joy than their struggles.

To have more control over what information I consume online, I have shut down the push notification feature for most of my mobile apps, and I am also more intentional when using my mobile phone. Rather than pick up the phone and start using it mindlessly, I first ask myself, *What is my purpose for using the phone right now?* If you don't develop good habits in your use of technology, technology becomes just another channel for your mind to find more proof that you are not good enough for others. It also cultivates our habit of comparing ourselves with others, which is another habit that promotes loneliness and separation.

The Habit of Comparing Ourselves with Others

The ego thrives on separation—and comparison creates separation. It doesn't matter if it's a positive or negative comparison. When you compare yourself with others and you feel inferior, superior, or even equal in any way, you are separating yourself from others.

One comparison that often evokes loneliness is comparing our relationships with the relationships that other people have. We often question why we don't have what other people have or why they are closer to each other than with us. Regardless of what answer you come up with, it doesn't feel good. If you think it's because other people are more sociable or attractive than you, then you will feel inferior. If you believe you are more spiritual, richer, or smarter than others, and that's why people don't understand or like you, then you are likely to feel a sense of separation from others. Even if you see yourself as equal to another, you might feel it's unfair when they get something and you don't. You might even feel envious.

Another common comparison that makes us feel lonely is when we compare how much time and effort we put into a relationship. We believe it is always up to us to be available and initiate a chat or other contact. We are more interested in being friends with others than they are with us. But comparing how much we contribute to our relationships and judging someone else's effort doesn't bring us closer; it only makes us feel disconnected.

It's best not to compare, because comparing creates a need for justification, which can only make you feel worse.

Comparison is often unfair anyway, because there are a lot of biases and errors when we compare. When we compare, we often justify the outcome with our existing beliefs. Comparing is only used to support the negative beliefs we already have about ourselves and others. Furthermore, we often compare our insides with other people's outsides. We use what we feel inside and compare it with what appears on the outside of other people. Most of the time, we don't know what other people are going through. They might appear successful in their careers and marriages, but also feel lonely. Sometimes, our comparison is based on our imagination, not on what we actually observe. When we feel lonely, we imagine everyone else is having a good time with their friends. This only intensifies our feelings of loneliness. We have a tendency to imagine the best for other people and the worst for ourselves. We think we are the only ones struggling, when in reality, there are many people like us who share the same experience.

At the end of the day, what matters is not how close other people are with each other. It's how close and connected *you* are with other people. Their relationships with others should not affect your relationships with anyone. When we compare, we train ourselves to focus on what's missing and lacking in our life. Instead of comparing yourself to someone else, appreciate what you have right now and what you have to offer.

The Habit of Taking Things Personally

The ego loves to make everything personal. Taking things personally adds to the narrative and helps to strengthen the superior or inferior identity that the ego is building. All of the beliefs mentioned in the previous chapter can be traced back to some kind of negative self-perception. When we take things personally—thinking everything that goes wrong has something to do with us—our negative beliefs are activated and we feel lonely.

Other people's actions are usually more about them than about us. When someone doesn't contact us or return our texts, perhaps they are busy, absent-minded, or they have new priorities in life. Perhaps they are just not in the mood to talk to anyone and they need space, or they feel it's time to move on to another relationship. Whatever the case might be, it has nothing to do with us. We are not responsible for their actions and their perceptions. We cannot control what others do or how they think and feel about us. When we take things personally, not only do we start to judge ourselves, but we also blame others and set ourselves up as victims. Judging others and withholding our love causes us to disconnect from love.

The ego thrives on separation,

and what's a better way of creating separation

than to create enemies?

When somebody says or does something that hurts us, our minds are quick to call them a villain or a bad person. We often confuse other people's actions with who they are. People might have acted in ways that hurt us, but that doesn't mean they have bad intentions or they *intended* to hurt us.

For example, once a reader criticized my writing and her choice of words was harsh. She used words such as "anal," "cocky," and "repulsive." I knew she had good intentions. She was just trying to help me become a better writer, but this doesn't take away the fact that I felt hurt. So

I wrote to her and explained how I felt, and how my dad used to criticize me in order to motivate me, and how it only made me feel bad about myself. I also told her that I don't believe harsh words are necessary when giving feedback to another person. She replied and told me her childhood was similar to mine and she never intended to hurt me. English isn't her first language and what she meant might have been lost in translation. If I were to judge her and consider her to be an ill-meaning person right from the start, I would have missed this opportunity to connect with my reader on a deeper level.

Judging others also prevents us from healing our pain. It might feel good when we have someone to blame. But in doing so we have missed the chance to self-reflect and uncover the emotional pain that is buried deep within us. Your emotions give you information about yourself. They don't give you information about other people. When you feel lonely, you are holding onto some mental perception that is blocking you from feeling love. What other people do is secondary. More often than not, they only reactivate the pain you are already carrying. If you feel hurt or triggered by other people's actions, you probably experienced something similar in the past that you haven't resolved yet. Other people's actions are about them, but our reaction to their actions is about us.

The Habit of Seeking Approval from Others

As humans, we all have an innate desire to belong. Most of us learned in adolescence that we have to follow the group norm, act like everyone else, and accommodate others to fit in with the group. Sometimes, due to peer pressure, we are persuaded to do something we don't normally do, or don't want to do. Even if it's unspoken, we still feel the pressure to conform because of our fear of rejection and exclusion.

However, fitting in is not the same as belonging. We don't feel like we belong when we have to sacrifice our authentic self to gain approval from others. When we cannot be and express ourselves completely, we feel disconnected and lonely inside. Whether it's a group setting or a one-to-one relationship, any time you please others at the expense of your truth, you are sending yourself the message that you are not as important as the other person. Any time you put up a front or change who you are to fit in, you are abandoning yourself in the process.

True acceptance doesn't require you to

fit in or change who you are.

It doesn't have to be sought; it's given to you.

I used to feel lonely because I felt like I didn't fit in. When I was in secondary school, I was a quiet, nerdy kid who loved to read. The other boys in my school were more active and rowdy. I found it difficult to get along with them. I felt like I had to give up my introverted personality and my interest in reading in order to fit in. But I didn't want to. I would rather be rejected by my peers than compromise in this way.

Now, I realize there is no need to fit in or seek approval from others. I can just be myself and validate myself. This is enough. Plus, friends who truly love and accept you will embrace and appreciate your unique self-expression. They will not pressure or force you to change or do something that you dislike. Fitting in requires you to change, but true acceptance doesn't. If you have to pretend to be someone else in order to feel accepted by others, then any acceptance you receive is inauthentic. They do not truly appreciate who you are. You are only accepted if you conform to the image they project onto you. So maybe it's time to move on and consider other groups.

Furthermore, acceptance should be given freely. We shouldn't have to beg, manipulate, earn, or seek it. You can't force other people to accept you when they don't. The reason we are in the habit of seeking approval is we think people will accept us if we become what they want us to be. This is a strategy that most of us learned to get love from our parents when we were young. We think we need to be what our parents want us to be in order to be loved by them. But this is conditional love, and if we overdo it, we are in danger of developing the habit of neglecting ourselves and we lose touch with our true desires and purpose.

The Habit of Keeping Our Guard Up

The ego protects us from being hurt by others. But if this gets too extreme, we will develop trust issues and find it difficult to connect with anyone at a deeper level. Examples of keeping our guard up include: withdrawing when we feel hurt; keeping an emotional distance by not sharing too much about ourselves; or trying to appear perfect in front of others by projecting the image we want others to see.

Social conditioning tells us it's inappropriate to share our struggles and emotional pain with others. We don't wish to appear needy, incompetent, or be a burden. So we show the parts of ourselves we think are acceptable and hide the parts we are ashamed of. Men, in particular, feel somewhat ashamed to talk about their emotions and problems with others because they are afraid of appearing weak. We are taught to act tough and mask our insecurities. People with mental illness and those who suffer from trauma such as abuse, keep silent and don't talk about their struggles because they don't feel safe sharing their experiences.

But being silent doesn't mean we are strong. We might appear strong, but if we are pretending to be happy we are not being true to ourselves or anyone else. The more we protect our hearts and hide our struggles, the more we feel disconnected. Other people don't have an opportunity to understand us and what we are going through, unless we open up.

Keeping everything to ourselves
makes us feel like we are the only ones
who experience struggle.

When we close ourselves to others, we feel isolated from the world and the people around us. When we open up, we give other people permission to do the same. We offer them a chance to love and support us. Five years ago, I had a breakdown when I shared my childhood experiences of low self-esteem during a presentation. After the presentation, my friends came up to me individually to show support. Some asked if I was okay. Some said I was courageous and authentic. The most touching moment was when I received a note from a friend who told me that he also had low self-esteem when he was young. I always knew other people had low self-esteem, but to hear it from someone else—especially a friend I perceived as confident and successful—allowed me to feel more connected to him and to myself.

Of course, before we can open up to others, we have to first connect deeply with our own emotions and thoughts and process them. Sharing what we think and feel is not the same as sharing how others make us think and feel. One is about taking responsibility, while the other is about blaming someone else. If we aren't responsible for our own emotions and thoughts, we can't have a meaningful conversation with anyone else. What we share will sound more like complaints, venting, or sob stories. This only turns people off and attracts other complainers or victims into our lives.

PART 3

Staying Connected

Chapter 8

Changing the Ego's Story

"We must rewrite our story from one of fear to one of celebration."

— KAMERON HURLEY, RAPTURE

In my book, *Empty Your Cup*, I shared the movie analogy: Our spiritual self is like an audience watching the movie; our mind is like the director who makes the movie, and our body is like an actor who carries out the instructions given by the director.

When we don't have awareness of our spiritual self, we are completely identified with the story created by the mind. We are so absorbed by the "movie" that we forget we are the audience and not the characters in the movie. Even if the story makes us feel lonely, we continue to watch the movie and believe the story is true, because there is no space between the movie and the audience.

However, once we become conscious of our spiritual nature, we realize that we are observers perceiving events in our life just as we are the audience watching a movie. We know the movie is mind-made and we are no longer identified with the story. If a movie is not worth watching, as an audience, we can choose not to watch it.

As an audience,
we get to choose the movie we want to watch.

When you feel lonely, acknowledge your emotion and allow yourself to feel it, rather than seeing it as something you have to fix or get rid of. See it as a choice you need to make. What movie do you want to watch? A movie about loneliness and separation, or a movie about love and connection? When you are sick of the same, old melancholy movie that is playing in your mind, you will naturally want to change the story. And if you have an awareness of how your ego creates the stories, you can break down the structure bit by bit.

Here's how I did it.

First I set about changing my behavioral habits. For

me, this was the easiest to do. As mentioned before, I shut down all the push notifications for social media and messengers. I changed the settings on my social media to have better control of what posts I see on my newsfeed. I put away my mobile phone in the morning and did not check my messages until noon. The purpose of making these minor tweaks and changes was to reduce the number of trigger points and events that could activate my ego to tell its stories. I want to use my mobile when I intend to use it, not whenever there is a notification alert.

The second thing I did was to interrupt my mind from interpreting events in the same way all the time. As mentioned in Chapter 5, events don't affect us, but rather the meaning we attached to them does. Now I'm more mindful of which events trigger my ego to tell its stories. And whenever these events occur, I just notice the interpretation and then I drop it immediately. For example, when my mind starts to justify why someone doesn't reply to my text, I tell myself: *I don't need to know why someone didn't respond to my text. It is what it is.* Then, I continue with my life. I understand that no matter what justification my mind comes up with—whether it's my fault or someone else's fault—it only brings disconnection, so it's best not to interpret events. Without interpretation, events can't do us any harm.

Of course, it's not easy to change our mental habits overnight. The interpretation of events is supported by our beliefs, which are usually formed and carried forward from childhood. So there is already a momentum to interpret events in the same way. It will take some time and a lot of practice for the mind to get used to not interpreting events in this way. Sometimes, it's easier to remove your psychological blocks by changing your perspective regarding old events or by introducing a new belief.

In my case, the belief that has kept me stuck is: *No one wants to be my friend.* As I examined deeper, I realized my underlying belief is: *I'm not significant and important enough.* This belief was created way back when I was emotionally neglected as a child and my parents failed to notice I needed attention. To neutralize the charges from these stories, I started telling myself over and over, many times a day: *I'm significant; I'm important; and I matter.* Whenever I say this, I pause and allow the feeling to enter my heart. It has become my new mantra. Whenever I notice events that can trigger feelings of loneliness, I repeat this mantra before my ego has a chance to tell its story. If you keep telling your mind the same thing over and over again, it will start to take on the new belief and overwrite the old belief in the process.

It doesn't matter where you start.

As long as you change the meaning you've assigned to events, the ego's story will ultimately change.

Even though I start first with habits and events, and then beliefs, you don't have to follow this same sequence. You can start from events or beliefs first. Go for the one that is the easiest for you. The key thing is to change all three components of the story structure so the ego's story gets weakened significantly. You might have to go back to the start of the sequence and repeat it many times with a different set of events, beliefs, and habits, until the story completely loses its charge.

Questions to Help You Change the Story

In the previous chapters, we have explored some of the common events, beliefs, and habits that evoke loneliness. But being aware of them is only the first step. To rewrite the story, we have to ask empowering questions that enable the stories to be rewritten. We want to examine our past and our current habits from a place of stillness, curiosity, and non-judgment. Otherwise, we might start analyzing our past and get drawn back into the ego's repetitive stories.

Below are some questions you can ask yourself as you go about changing the ego's story. You can ask these questions during meditation or self-reflection, when you tend to be more present. It doesn't matter if you have the answers immediately, or not. The answers will be revealed to you through insights or events in the future, as you keep asking the questions.

1. How would I perceive an event if I can't blame anyone?

When we are in victim consciousness, we look for someone to blame. We ask ourselves disempowering questions such as: *What's wrong with me? Who is to blame for this?* and *Why did they do this to me?* But asking disempowering questions only gives you disempowering answers. For example, when you ask what's wrong with you, clearly you are seeking a negative aspect of yourself to justify a specific event. When you ask yourself why you are always alone, your answers will always come from your existing negative beliefs and end up being something like: *No one cares about me,* or *I don't fit in anywhere.* Whatever answers you get, it will not make you feel good.

Asking yourself the right question is very important. Instead of seeking someone to blame for our misfortune, we can ask ourselves: *If nobody is at fault here and I couldn't blame someone else, or myself, for this event, how would I perceive this event?* For example, you ask someone out and they don't reply to your text. Do you blame the other person for ignoring you and not making an effort to maintain the friendship? Do you blame yourself for not being desirable and interesting enough? Or do *you just perceive the event as it is* without the need to justify other people's actions or your worth? You ask someone out and they don't respond. That's it. End of story. No justification is needed. Only the ego needs to attribute blame to someone, because it helps strengthen the story it's building.

2. How can I perceive a particular event differently, now that I'm an adult?

Many of our beliefs are formed during childhood, which is usually limited and not beneficial to us anymore. So ask yourself, *If I could perceive a past event from the perspective of adulthood, how could I (as an adult) perceive it differently?* Asking yourself this question can help you identify any outdated beliefs you are still holding onto.

For example, I used to feel unimportant because my

mom had no time to help me with my spelling. But now, as an adult, I can see why. I was so independent that my mom didn't need to pay much attention to me. I kind of replaced my mom with a tape recorder when I used it to record my voice and help myself with my spelling. Her lack of attention doesn't mean I didn't matter or she doesn't love me.

Also, understanding that you were helpless and mostly powerless when you first formed your beliefs will allow you to have compassion for the little girl or boy you once were, and love the inner child still residing within you. You will start to understand that these events have nothing to do with how good or bad you were as a child, and you can choose to let go of the negative self-beliefs you first formed in childhood.

3. What can I learn from the events in my life?

When you believe every event that occurs in your life serves the purpose of helping you grow and expand, you will see it from a different perspective. Instead of resisting the events that occur, you will begin to extract value from all your life experiences and become more appreciative of them. For example, in my case, even though Pat reminded me of James and brought out tremendous insecurity, pain, resentment in me, I'm grateful to have known him. If it wasn't for him, I wouldn't have been reminded of my past, and I wouldn't have been given the chance to process my unresolved emotions and learn to practice forgiveness.

Whenever an event triggers feelings of loneliness in you, ask yourself, *What is this event trying to teach me? What message is this event trying to convey? What lesson can I learn from it? What good does this experience bring? How will it help me grow?* Asking these questions will help you in your transformation. They can direct your mind in seeking insights and prevent you from ruminating about the past.

The answers to these types of questions will tell you how you can perceive experiences differently when similar events occur. Then, in the future, you can change your reactions and the outcome of what happens in your life. When you don't react to these events the same way you did previously, the triggers that activate the ego's story will no longer be triggers. Without these triggers, the ego will have fewer opportunities to tell its stories.

4. How can I learn to feel the love that is already within me?

In Chapter 6, we asked the question: *What am I thinking right now that is preventing me from feeling the love and connection that I desire?* This question can help us uncover the hidden beliefs that cause us to feel lonely.

After you uncover your hidden beliefs, ask yourself: *Can I let this belief go? What do I need to believe or tell myself so I can feel the love that is already within me?* It could be beliefs such as: *I am enough; I am worthy and deserving of love just like everyone else;* or *I am love. I'm connected to the Source of love.*

You can also ask yourself: *How can I perceive myself and others in a better light?* So for example, if someone hurts you, thinking they are ignorant, unconscious, or disconnected from their soul brings you closer to the love within you than assuming they are deliberately and intentionally harming you. Thinking the latter only creates an enemy out of the other person and causes separation, which is what the ego needs to tell its stories.

5. What did I need to hear as a child?

As children, no matter how loving our parents are, we might still end up with emotional wounds, unmet needs, and limiting beliefs. Growing up, most of us unconsciously transfer the responsibility to meet these unmet emotional needs from our parents to our friends and partners. We depend on others to make us feel happy, included, and loved.

When you feel lonely, ask yourself: *What do I want from other people, and how do I want them to make me feel? How can I give these feelings to myself?* The things you want from other people now are most likely the things you have been wanting since childhood. Instead of waiting for others to fulfill your needs, take full responsibility for your unmet needs. Give yourself what you want from others, and tell yourself what you have always wanted to hear as a child.

I know that as a child, I didn't feel like I mattered, and I felt even more so when I was a teenager in school. I always depended on other people to give me attention and make me feel important. But now, with an awareness of my unmet childhood needs, I started telling myself: *I'm significant, I'm important, and I matter.* After some time, I started feeling good enough on my own and self-sufficient. I don't need others to validate my importance anymore, and I don't feel lonely that often when other people ignore or don't have time for me. It still feels good when other people listen to me attentively when I speak, but now this is just a bonus, because I'm already there for my inner child and have taken care of its needs.

6. Why do I connect with others so effortlessly?

When we feel lonely, we often seek justification as to why

we ended up in an unhappy state. As mentioned in the first question, when you approach loneliness in this way, you receive disempowering answers that can cause you to sink deeper into loneliness. Instead of asking yourself: *Why doesn't anyone want to be my friend?*, flip the question around and ask yourself: *Why do people want to be my friends? Why are people so interested in me? Why do I connect with others so effortlessly? Why do I feel so included in the group?*

When you ask such questions, you direct your mind to look for positive aspects of yourself. You begin to see things you never saw in yourself before, and you start to appreciate the good qualities you possess. We all want to acknowledge our feelings of loneliness, but we don't want to focus on it too much, because focusing on loneliness doesn't help us get out of loneliness. It only activates the ego to tell more stories of separation and we end up feeling lonelier. It's only when we let go of our loneliness and focus on something more positive that we start to experience joy, love, and appreciation.

7. What habits can I develop to help me feel more connected?

Being aware of our habits is not enough. Many people are aware of their bad habits but they still do them. First, they might have some hidden, negative self-beliefs that still support these habits. Second, they focus too much on stopping themselves from acting a certain way, which only causes more resistance and craving to act.

A better way of changing our habits is to create a new habit to replace the old one. You can add new habits that help you connect deeper with your spirit, such as meditation, breathing exercises, taking a walk in the neighborhood or nature, and journaling. If something causes you to feel lonely, make it a habit to think of something else. Like in my case, the events that make me feel lonely used to be a trigger for my ego to tell its story. Now, these events have become a trigger for more positive thoughts. Instead of entertaining the story my ego tells me, I immediately tell myself: *I'm significant, I'm important, and I matter.*

Also, see if you can make minor tweaks to your lifestyle and environment, especially how you use technology. For example, when I'm at home, I usually put my mobile phone out of reach. So if I want to use it, I need to stand up and go get it. This gives me some buffer time to be clear of my intention before using the phone. If someone keeps triggering your feelings of loneliness, you might consider changing your communication style with them, spending less time with them, or even ending your relationships with them. It's difficult to grow when the habits you want to change are constantly triggered by the people around you.

Dealing With Resistance From the Ego

When you grow and try to change your story, your ego will resist. Understand this is normal. The ego is very attached to the old stories and programming. It doesn't want to let them go. It's just like how we keep a backup of all our old documents in our hard drive, or accumulate more and more possessions. Even though most of the documents and possessions are not useful to us anymore, we don't want to delete them or throw them away. We keep them just in case we might need them in the future. Similarly, we hold onto past events, beliefs, and habits because they have guided us for years. We feel insecure about letting the past go all at once.

Due to resistance from the ego, sometimes we feel worse during our time of transformation. We might experience periods of moodiness, resentment, and restlessness. We become stuck and overwhelmed. We might experience withdrawal symptoms when we remove or change our habits. Some of us might even hit the lowest point in our lives, when everything seems to be falling apart and meaningless. The ego seeks an identity from the stories it has created. When we change the fundamental structure of the ego, suddenly everything is turned upside down and nothing makes sense anymore. Everything we used to strive for seems meaningless and pointless. It will take some time for us to adjust and find new meaning in life.

Think about this: If you have always derived your identity from your relationships and getting love from others — but now you realize that other people cannot make you feel less lonely, and that seeking love from others is no longer a strategy that works — what is left for your ego to do? It suddenly becomes jobless. The part of your identity that depended on others will then have to die. So your ego will do its best to prevent you from growing and to keep the status quo.

After I started feeling more self-sufficient, I decided to spend less time in groups or with people who didn't interest or resonate with me anymore. But instead of feeling better, I felt resentful towards them. I didn't understand why. It was my choice to move on and I did it for my spiritual growth. Yet, there was this persistent voice inside my head that needed to justify why I had to leave and also blame them for causing me to leave.

Months later, I finally realized it was because I felt guilty about leaving them, even though it was for my growth. In my mind, I thought they would judge me for abandoning them, so I had to deflect the blame back onto them. But in reality, no one is judging me. At least, not in person. I was just judging myself. My whole life, I've believed I am insignificant and unimportant. Whenever I had a conflict with other people, my mom always advised me, "Don't ruin your relationship with others. Just bear with it." I was trained to feel bad and guilty for focusing on my own needs and desires. Subconsciously, I adopted the belief that I need to sacrifice myself, give up my desires, and do what I'm told, if I want to maintain harmonious relationships with others. If I choose my desires over my relationships, I feel as though I'm ruining my relationships. This is why I felt resentment towards others. I didn't feel I had the freedom to choose what I wanted. Deep down inside, I felt obligated to please others above myself.

After I became aware of this hidden belief and my feelings about it, I had to constantly assure myself it was okay to move on: *People will understand eventually. They will be fine. It will be better for both parties.* I had to direct my mind towards more meaningful activities and relationships that are aligned with my soul. If not, my "jobless" ego will start to create new problems for me to solve.

**When you are in a growth period,
know that when you understand the big picture,
you will feel better.**

Most of us have some stuck energy in our bodies and hidden beliefs that have not been uncovered yet. As we progress, more will be revealed to us, and with a new understanding, we will feel better.

It's difficult to embody the changes all at once. So work on it a bit at a time and take it slow. Sometimes, you might want to give up and return to your old habits or stories. That's okay, too. There's no shame in it. When you feel better and ready to give it another go, ask yourself: *Is this story, belief, or habit worth holding onto? What do I gain from holding onto it?* and then continue where you left off.

Finally, whenever the same old story returns and I feel stuck, I also like to ask myself: *Love or fear? Connection or separation? Peace or resentment?* It works like a charm, and it seems I always choose the positive over the negative. These short questions help disrupt the story immediately and empower you to choose. They prompt you to choose the type of "movie" you want to watch. It's an invitation to release everything that no longer serves you.

Chapter 9

Deepening Our Connection to Love

"I never found the companion that was so companionable as solitude."

— HENRY DAVID THOREAU, WALDEN

In November 2019, I went to Labrador Park in Singapore and spent three hours there alone, as suggested by a friend. During my time in the park, I was instructed to not wander around and explore. I was supposed to sit in one place and write down the thoughts that arose in my mind. I was told this exercise would help me gain clarity about what I want.

Right from the start, I wanted to know about relationships. So I asked myself: *Do I want a romantic relationship?* The answer was "No." Still not convinced, I asked the question a few more times. I even changed the question slightly: *Am I running away from relationships?* and *Am I afraid of having a relationship?* But every time I asked, the answer was always a very firm, clear "No." Finally, after several inquiries, a different answer arose: *At least not at this moment. You don't have the desire right now. You are looking for growth instead.*

What kind of growth? I asked with great curiosity.

You want a deeper connection with your true essence, my inner voice responded.

After an hour and a half of questions and answers on other topics, no more thoughts arose. The thinking mind had stopped completely. There was nothing else to do and nothing to ask. There was only nature and me. The rest of my time in the park, I simply sat on the bench and was one with all of life. I felt bliss, joy, acceptance, love, peace, freedom, appreciation, and aliveness. There was no sense of separation or loneliness.

Loneliness is an invitation to go deeper into our being. It wakes us up to the wholeness and completeness we already are.

My quiet reflection in the park helped me realize that I

often approach relationships from a place of lack and fear. Whenever I feel unwanted or my relationships end in disappointment, I soon attach myself to another person or a group and start to become idealistic about the new relationship. I try to find my significance through others, but this approach always fails. No human can make me feel important all the time. Trying to control others and their actions only makes me feel more frustrated, disconnected, and unaligned with love. Subconsciously, I feel incomplete and yearn for someone else to fill up what's missing in me. But the truth is no one can complete me, because I'm already complete in the first place. I just fail to recognize it.

Loneliness tells us that we have become oblivious to our intrinsic nature of wholeness and completeness. It calls us to wake up to the perfection that we already are. The deep connection we desire doesn't come from other people. It comes from deep within when we connect to our true essence. Our soulmate can't exist when we are not connected with our soul. It's impossible to have a deep connection with another person when we are not deeply connected with ourselves.

Everything begins with us.

The most important relationship is the relationship we have with ourselves, not the other relationships we long for. Sometimes, when we become too attached or dependent on others for love, our relationships can distract us from our relationship with ourselves.

After that day in the park, I took a break from my social life to cultivate a deeper spiritual life. I left all the social groups I was involved with in order to spend more time in solitude and connect with my deepest essence. I wanted to solidify the connection with my spirit, before I connected with others again. I wanted to connect with others from a place of love, not from a place of fear.

Fear Is Not the Same as Love

To deepen our connection to love, we must first understand what love is—and what love is not. Fear and love are not the same and they cannot coexist. Love brings people closer together, but fear pushes them apart. When you are connected to fear, you are automatically disconnected from love. But we often mistake fear for love.

For example, the reader I mentioned in Chapter 1 wants to get married and have children. Even though she wants love, she's approaching her relationship from a place of lack and fear of being judged. When you are alone and you want someone to be in a relationship with you — and you are desperate — you are not giving off the energy of love. Instead, you are telling yourself and others that you are incomplete on your own and you need the other person to make you feel better. The anxious energy you give off pushes potential partners and friends away and increases your feeling of loneliness.

When someone wants to end a relationship with us and we say, "I *love* you. Please don't leave me. I can't live without you," we are not expressing love. We are, however, expressing our fear of losing someone we *think* we love. Attaching ourselves to another person is nowhere near love. It's the egoic fear of being alone and abandoned. True love is without attachment and conditions. You don't need others to be with you to feel love. Unconditional love is a constant, stable flow of goodness. On the other hand, love that comes with conditions is reactive. It takes you up and down like a rollercoaster. When you attach yourself to someone else, your mood gets dragged along by their actions and inaction. When they do something you want them to do, you feel love, and when they don't, you don't feel love.

When we see others getting close to our object of

affection and we feel jealous or threatened, this is also not what love is. Whatever we cling tightly to or hoard eventually dies of suffocation, be it a flower or a relationship. Another person is not a possession we can hold onto forever. We have to let them go one day. Furthermore, love is all-inclusive. You can't ask the sun to shine for you and not shine on others. You can't be the only person that matters in the other person's life and ask them to give you all their attention.

Sometimes, we doubt our partner's intentions and analyze their actions, looking for any evidence they are going to leave us for someone else. Our beliefs are based on fear and insecurity, not love. When we protect ourselves and close our hearts for others, we think we are loving ourselves. But this is the fear of being hurt, not love. By putting our walls up, we prevented ourselves from receiving and giving love. We block love from flowing freely.

Even when we do something to help another, we might be acting from a place of fear, too. Some of us are afraid that if we don't please the other person, they will not love us. We help because we want to feel needed by others. On the other hand, some of us help others because we are worried they can't do something as well as we can. But worrying about someone is not love; it's a form of fear. We are trying to control the situation to avoid feeling afraid.

Ask yourself: "At this moment, am I approaching others from a place of fear or a place of love?"

Love is not about what you do or don't do. When you look into someone's eyes with presence, there is love. At that moment, you are one with the other person. You see yourself in the other person. You know that deep inside the other person there is a spiritual being, too, just like you. When you are connected spiritually in this way, there is nothing more you need to do to feel love for another. However, most of us are conditioned to earn love. We are brought up with conditional love. We think we have to do what our parents expect of us in order to feel we deserve love. In addition, we don't feel comfortable receiving love without doing something in exchange or meeting certain criteria.

Love is also not about our intentions. Someone might say they will love you forever, and they mean it at the moment they say it. But they might have a bad day and say something mean to you tomorrow. It's not that they don't have the intention to love you; they are just disconnected from love at that moment.

Love is all about our connection and alignment with our deep essence.

I love you when I'm connected to the love within. I don't love you when I'm not connected to the love within. We can be connected or disconnected, loving or unloving, depending on each moment. Love is always there and available to us. It is permanent within us, but our connection to love is not. That's why love always seems fleeting because our connection to love is fleeting. Our feelings of love can be turned into fear very quickly when we are not deeply rooted in presence and love. When our minds start to interfere and we believe the story it tells us of blame, insecurity, and fear, then there will be "you" and "me." At that moment, there will be separation, not oneness.

Most of us find it difficult to sustain our connection with love for very long. We forget and lose connection with Source as we go about our day. This is why spiritual practice is key, and one of the best spiritual practices is the practice of solitude.

The Practice of Solitude

It seems counterintuitive to practice solitude, especially when we feel lonely and long to be with someone. However, it's precisely our strong desire to seek love from others that makes the practice of solitude so important. Having a desire for love is never a problem. It's the incessant seeking of love outside of us that creates loneliness.

Most of us don't know how to consciously feel the love from within. We do it unconsciously through other people. Our alignment with love is always dependent on other people, which means we have no control over when we feel love — because we have no control over other people. Others can't be exactly the way we want them to be, at least not all the time. They are also not responsible for meeting our expectations or satisfying our lack of connection. Even if they want to, they can't.

When you feel love in someone's presence, the other person is not responsible for the love you feel — you are. You are the one who let go of your psychological blocks and allowed love to flow within you at that moment. It might seem as though the other person has some magical power that makes you fall for them. However, the truth is other people don't have the power to *control* how we think and feel. They can't make us feel love if we don't want to. We decide who we feel safe enough with to surrender and open our hearts. At best, other people can only *influence* our perception. Ultimately, it's our *choice* how we want to perceive our experiences. If we choose to hold onto the ego's story and block ourselves from love, there's nothing much others can do about it.

Others cannot do our inner work for us.

We have to do it ourselves.

The practice of solitude is a step towards taking responsibility for our inner alignment and taking back the power we have given away. We are not waiting for others to love us or make us feel complete. Instead, we get in touch with our spiritual selves and intentionally seek union within to feel love and our completeness. Best of all, we can do this anytime we want.

The practice of solitude is so important, because stepping away from people helps break our attachment to them. I realize that merely telling myself that I'm significant is not enough. I have this unyielding desire to be noticed, and I tend to get emotionally attached to others too quickly when they pay attention to me. But this habit often makes me feel unimportant instead of significant, because I continue to focus on others, even when they have stopped paying attention to me.

It's easier to go within when you are alone than with another person. When I'm with others, I tend to get carried away by their energy and lose my sense of self. I'm easily influenced by how I think other people will perceive me. I often define myself through others. To be certain that I'm listening to my inner voice and not my ego, I have to put my social life on hold, get away from all distractions, and ask myself, *Who am I without my relationships? How can I be significant without depending on others? How can I love others without being attached to them? Are my actions influenced by what other people think of me? Are my actions really what I intend to do, or are they what someone else wants me to do?*

By spending time alone, I make sure there is no one to turn to but my spirit.

Solitude is where true love, significance, and connection lies. When we embrace and accept solitude, loneliness dissolves.

There is an abundance of love around you and within you. The three hours I spent in the park being with myself was the most amazing time, an experience I could never find with another person. No one can ever match it. The love I am seeking is deep within me. And when I connect with it, I connect to something larger and more significant than my egoic self. I feel deeply connected to all life in the cosmos. I feel a deep sense of belonging to the Universe, which I rarely feel in another person, group, or community. I know that I'm supported and I'm not alone on my journey through life.

But to access this deep connection within, you need to practice solitude. It's necessary for spiritual connection and transformation. A caterpillar needs to hide in the cocoon before it can morph into a butterfly. When you are redefining yourself, it's best to spend time alone.

Being around other people while you are evolving can confuse them, because they are familiar with your old self and will relate to you in the same ways they always have.

But you are not the same as before. You might be easily annoyed, which could hurt your relationships. It's only when you have transformed and are certain of your new spiritual identity that you can begin to relate to others in new ways.

How to Practice Solitude

First of all, the practice of solitude is intentional. Unlike when we feel lonely and isolated by others, we choose a preferred time to be alone. Withdrawing from others because we feel hurt by them is not to be mistaken for practicing solitude. The former is about protection, separation, and fear, while the latter is about openness, connection, and love. You are not getting away from people because you secretly hope they will notice your absence. Solitude is not a tool to manipulate others to pay attention to you.

Solitude is also not just about being physically alone. You want to remove all distractions, such as your phone and other electronic devices, in order to truly connect with your true self. When you are alone, you also don't want to have mental chatter, let your mind wander away, or keep yourself occupied with activities. You want to be present and free from the mental and physical dimensions as much as possible so you can be in touch with the spiritual dimension. Your practice of solitude begins when your ego has nothing to grab onto or attach itself to.

Being alone is just one component.

The practice of solitude usually includes some focus on silence and stillness.

There are several ways you can practice solitude. If you combine all three components (solitude, silence, and stillness), you will have a formal sitting meditation where you sit down on the floor in a cross-legged position or on a chair. During meditation, let go of any thoughts that arise and simply focus on your breathing. You can choose to close or open your eyes, depending on what helps you stay connected.

If you find it difficult to keep still while meditating, you can try walking meditation, instead. As you walk slowly from one destination to another, be mindful of your breath and the contact of your feet with the ground as you take each step. Walking in nature also helps us to open up space within and connect to love easily. You can use your five senses to appreciate the beauty of nature. Don't listen to any music or other audio and avoid having a dialogue in your mind while you walk. Give your complete attention to your surroundings and your body. Feel the same spaciousness that exists within you and in nature. Even though walking meditation focuses on solitude and silence, you will also feel a sense of inner stillness when you connect deeply with the surroundings and your body in this way.

Alternatively, you can combine solitude and stillness, and focus more on these two components. When I was in the park, I wasn't meditating or training my mind to be silent. I was asking questions and allowing my spirit to provide me with the answers. You can connect to love even during deep contemplation, self-reflection, or journaling. Simply bring down the volume of your analytical mind so you can hear the voice deep within. You are not actively thinking about something or finding a solution to your problems. Instead, after you ask a question, pause and wait patiently for the answer. It's more about listening than seeking an answer. Even though silence might not be the main focus here, you will experience silence in the space between the question and the answer. After a while, you might realize there are no more questions to ask. When this moment comes, simply relax and enjoy your beingness and connection with love.

To truly reap the benefits of being with yourself, it's good to practice solitude for an extended period. You don't have to be like me and sit in the park for three hours. Even though I like to be alone, I faced huge resistance at the beginning of this practice. My mind would come up with all kinds of excuses to not go to the park. So start small, instead. For example, find a quiet spot in your home, set a timer, and spend five to fifteen minutes a day in solitude. Most importantly, create consistency in your practice of solitude. Five minutes each day is better than three hours a week. A couple of years ago, even before my friend's suggestion, I went to other parks once or twice a month. But life gets busy and I stopped going. Now that I am reminded of the importance of solitude, I just keep to my daily practices at home. If I want more time to be with myself, then I go to the park.

Establish an "Inner Home" You Can Always Return to

Practicing solitude doesn't mean we don't care about our relationships or we avoid interacting with others. But reconnecting with ourselves is always the starting point. Taking care of our alignment is a higher priority that takes precedence over connecting with others.

According to the Zen Master Thich Nhat Hanh, there is an order of connection. We must learn how to connect with our highest self before we can connect deeply with another individual, and then we can collectively connect with a group. Without the first step of connecting with yourself, the second step is not possible. He uses the analogy of a "home" inside of us to represent this deep connection with our true essence.

You will never feel at home when you are constantly looking for your home outside of yourself.

When two people have individual homes and they are whole in themselves, then together they can form a collective home. After this, they will be able to invite more people into their home and connect with them deeply. This is what a real relationship is. We are not here to complete each other. We are here to *remind* each other that we are complete. If you try to lean on others when they do not have a strong home, or they try to lean on you when you don't have a strong home, then both of your homes will collapse and the relationship will become dysfunctional.

When we practice solitude for a long time, we can

establish a stable home within. Even when we go out and interact with the world, we won't get easily swayed or influenced by other people and external circumstances. But we don't have to wait until we are fully complete before we connect with others, because we can never be completely ready. We'll still get disconnected from time to time. Moreover, it's only through our interactions with others that we get to test how strong our inner home really is.

It's not about staying connected all the time.
What's important is to have an inner home
you can return to.

If you are aware of the sacred space and love within you, every time you feel lonely or disconnected there will be an inner home waiting for you. Instead of manipulating someone to love you, train yourself to return to your home, and connect to the spiritual dimension within. The repetition of returning home will make your home stronger. Once you have established a strong home within, you will experience a sense of calmness and presence instead of neediness and inadequacy when you approach others. All parties will then enjoy their time together even more.

Interacting with others is a dynamic process. You shift and adjust your energy according to the circumstances. When you are connecting with others, you have to focus a little bit more on the other person. If not, you will appear uninterested, self-centered, and aloof. However, you also don't go all the way out and put all your energy on the other person. You will still have to maintain some focus on yourself while interacting with others. Your inner home still has to be the priority. If not, you will find yourself highly impressionable. When the conversation ends, you have to reel in all your energy and return home. You don't leave your energy dangling out there while yearning for the other person to come back to you, because this will create more loneliness.

Chapter 10

Deepening Our Connection With Others

"Very often in a conflict, we believe the problem is the other person or group. But looking deeply, we know that we are not the only ones who have suffered — they have also suffered."

— THICH NHAT HANH

One night, I had a dream: I saw three of my friends on the street and I approached them to say "Hi." But instead of returning my greeting, they immediately turned around and walked away. I quickly stopped them and said, "Hey, what's wrong?" None of them said a word. I looked at one of my friends and he started crying. I looked at another friend and he started crying, too. In my dream, I realized they felt hurt by me, but I was rather confused. I didn't know what I had done wrong.

One of them finally explained to me, "I feel like you have abandoned us, now that you have grown and changed. Whenever you talk about how great you feel in other groups, I feel hurt."

Still dreaming, I said, "No...I left the group because you formed a new group without me and you don't invite me to the gatherings anymore. I felt like I was being abandoned."

Knowing that my friends feel the same way I do, I felt compassionate towards them, and I gave each one a hug. As I hugged them, I woke up from my dream. All of the resentment I had been feeling towards my friends for months had been melted away by the tenderness created by my compassion. Now, I understand that when our friends or partner move away from us, we suffer a sense of betrayal, whether the other person has bad intentions, or not. Even if they are moving to a new country for a new job, it hurts, because what once was familiar to us is now gone. We all feel the same way when we become overly attached to other people and relationships.

Compassion melts away the animosity and separateness you feel towards others.

Compassion for others creates a deeper connection and brings you closer. Everyone has their side of the story. In our minds, we might think other people enjoy hurting us. But this is often untrue. When you can see past the stories of the ego and see the wound in both of you, it will be easier for you to forgive. I have been doing a lot of forgiving since I started writing this book. I didn't just forgive people who have hurt me, I also forgave myself for harboring resentment towards them and the harm I did to my body for holding onto these resentments.

Forgiveness and compassion set us free from the ego's stories and help us reopen our hearts to others. If we are waiting for someone to say "I'm sorry" to us so we can forgive them, we might never get it. People who realize they have hurt us might find it too shameful to apologize and admit what they have done. Others might have unintentionally hurt us without realizing it. From their perspective, they didn't do anything wrong. After forgiving James and the person I blamed for our drifting apart, I stumbled upon a photo of them together. Strangely, I felt at peace with the situation. They probably don't even know they hurt me, so why am I holding onto resentment? I am amazed that they still keep in contact with each other after so many years, and I wish the best for them.

When we forgive, it doesn't mean our relationships will return to what they were previously. Relationships dissolve and evolve. People change, grow, and move on. However, forgiveness brings us a step closer to the love within. It helps us let go of our part of the story and the need to justify or find someone to blame for our hurt feelings.

True spiritual love is all-encompassing and unconditional. When we are connected to love, we love everyone and all of life. We don't give love to only a selected few and withdraw our love from the rest. When we focus only on a few people, our perception of love is limited and based on conditions: *I will love you if you satisfy my needs or meet my criteria. I will love you only if you love me, too. You can only love me and no one else; otherwise, I won't love you anymore.*

In spirituality, this defies the true essence of love. Love is not a trade or an exchange of benefits. You can't be aligned to love without loving all beings. Any hostility you have for another person will disconnect you from the love within. When you embody love, it doesn't matter if someone deserves your love or not. You bless them anyway. You don't have to meet them again or continue a relationship with them, but you also don't need to hold any animosity towards them.

This is not always easy to do. But there is a practice called the Loving-Kindness Meditation that can help you get better at it.

Loving-Kindness Meditation

The Loving-Kindness Meditation can help us feel interconnected with other people and the world. The core of this practice is:

What you wish for yourself,

you wish for everyone else.

This works only if you have deep compassion for yourself first. If you don't love yourself, it's difficult to love others. This is why, as mentioned previously, it's important to establish your inner home first.

There are different variations to the Loving-Kindness Meditation, but all of them can help you extend your love beyond yourself and your loved ones. Below is a guide you can follow. You can change the words according to what resonates and feels most natural to you.

1. Find a quiet spot where you won't be disturbed. Close your eyes and focus on your breath. Breathe in through your nose and breathe out through your mouth. Release any tension in your body and go deeper each time with each breath. If any thoughts surface, let go of them as you take a new breath.

2. When you have reached a place of serenity and love, imagine the love flowing from your heart to the rest of your body — your arms, hands, legs, torso, head, and your inner organs. Feel the love circulating in your body for as long as you feel comfortable.

3. Recite the following to yourself:
    May I be happy. May I be well.
    May I be safe and healthy.

May I be peaceful and at ease.

4. Next, bring to mind someone you love and recite the following. Imagine that you are sending love to the other person.
    May you be happy. May you be well.
    May you be safe and healthy.
    May you be peaceful and at ease.

5. Then, bring to mind a neutral person. It could be a stranger or an acquaintance you don't have any special feelings about. Repeat the following and send love to the other person.
    May you be happy. May you be well.
    May you be safe and healthy.
    May you be peaceful and at ease.

6. Next, bring to mind someone you feel hostile towards or someone you have difficulty loving. Do the best you can to give them the same blessing.
    May you be happy. May you be well.
    May you be safe and healthy.
    May you be peaceful and at ease.

7. Finally, end the meditation by giving your blessing to all living beings. Many others experience the same pain as you. Wish them well.

May all beings be happy. May all beings be well.
May all beings be safe and healthy.
May all beings be peaceful and at ease.

8. Take a deep breath in. And as you breathe out, notice how you feel. When you are ready, open your eyes.

The Four Levels of Connection

We can connect with others on four different levels. The connection gets deeper at each level.

First, you can connect with others on a physical level. This includes touch, such as a handshake, a pat on the back, or a hug. It's about being physically there for another and feeling the warmth and support from others. Apart from physical affection, this level is also about doing activities together. We might share the same hobbies and interests with our friends. When we communicate at this level, we talk about what we see, hear, smell, taste, and touch. We share tangible information, such as the latest news, what we ate for lunch, or what we do for our holiday, without going too deeply into our experiences.

The second level of connection you can have with someone is the mental level. At this level, we share our ideas, beliefs, and knowledge with others. It's about having an intellectual conversation or discussion. What we share is usually something deeper than our sense perception. So instead of describing what you saw, you share your opinion about it. Listening to other people's thoughts and worldview can help stimulate your thinking, especially when someone shares a new perspective or asks you a question you have never thought of before.

Then, there is the third level of connection — the emotional connection. At this level, we share how we feel. Instead of protecting ourselves, we open up and allow ourselves to be vulnerable. We stop pretending to be perfect just to impress others. At this level of connection, we can have a deep, authentic conversation and feel free to share a wide range of our emotions — the negative and the positive ones — without feeling judged. When we connect with others at this level, we feel a sense of emotional closeness and intimacy with them.

Finally, the fourth level of connection, the deepest level at which we can connect, is the spiritual dimension. This is not just about connecting to a Higher Power. It is the connection to your spirit, your partner's spirit, and the spirit of every being on Earth. When you connect with others at this level, you are them and they are you. There is a deep knowing and oneness with the Universe and no trace of separation. Just pure joy, love, and peace.

**The first three levels of connection are
ever-changing and limiting.
Only the spiritual connection is
lasting and always available.**

The first three levels of connections signify the human aspects of who we are. They correspond to the body, mind, and heart connection. It feels great to connect with someone at the first three levels. They are what the ego craves. However, they are impermanent. Your partner and friends cannot be physically present with you all the time. Your thoughts and beliefs change as you grow. The friends you once shared the same worldview and beliefs with might have grown in a completely different direction. Emotional connection and intimacy also don't last. They can dissolve quickly when the people we once felt safe in sharing our emotions with do something that betrays our trust. The first three levels of connection are constantly changing and we suffer when we are attached to them.

Furthermore, the first three levels of connection are only limited to our friends and family. We choose who we feel comfortable and safe being around and sharing our thoughts and emotions. Often, only people who share common beliefs with us and those who understand our emotions are welcomed in. We also let people in only after spending more time with them, after trust has developed. At the first three levels, it's difficult to connect with someone who doesn't understand our point of view or our struggles. Some people might not have the same level of desire for these connections as we do. For example, those who are emotionally neglected usually crave more emotional connection than most people can offer. So we often feel a lack of connection with others.

On the other hand, when you are spiritually connected, you always feel like you have enough. You don't need more spiritual connections. You know the formless dimension is always there and readily available to us. It's eternal. It's not something we can grasp, so there's no fear of losing it. Even though the spiritual realm might be elusive for some people, we don't need others to understand and experience spirituality in order for us to be spiritually connected with them. Within, they are also spirit, just like us. We just need to look beyond their ego and surface personality, and tune into their spirit to connect with them spiritually.

Also, when we connect with others on the spiritual level, we can connect with anyone, even if they are strangers or enemies. The spiritual connection is not limited to our friends, family, and partners. If we can't connect with others at the fourth level, it just means we are not seeing them deeply enough.

How to Connect Spiritually

In building friendships, we gradually share more and more details about ourselves. This process creates trust between people. However, even though someone might tell you everything about themselves, their past, their hopes and aspirations, or show you their full personality and feelings, you don't *really* know the person. You only know them through your perception of them, which is usually based on what they do and what they share with you.

To know the true essence of someone, you need to see

beyond your mental perceptions and connect with them on a deeper, spiritual level. If not, what you see is merely a projection of the image your ego or someone else's ego wants you to see.

We get separated like the branches and leaves of a tree.

But if we go deeper,

we will realize we come from the same trunk.

At the level of form, we are all different. We are different in gender, race, size, nationality, religion, personality, opinions, beliefs, and more. But if we go deeper, we will realize that we are unique expressions of the same source that creates the whole universe. Most of us don't feel this deep connection with others because we fail to see that we are part of the same tree. We can only see how different we are from other people at the form level.

However, it's not easy to see others as spiritual beings. Knowing deeply about yourself doesn't always mean you know deeply about others, too. Certain people can cause us to react easily and this makes it difficult for us to see beyond the level of form. Similar to solitude, this takes practice. Here are four things you can do to develop a better spiritual connection with others:

1. Make more eye contact.

Eye contact builds more than a physical and emotional connection. It also helps us connect with others spiritually. There is a common saying, "The eyes are the windows of the soul." If you look deep enough into someone's eyes, you will feel the aliveness of their soul. This soul-to-soul connection is nonverbal and cannot be described in words. But you can feel the exchange of energy between two people through the eyes.

Even though technology helps us make more friends from other countries, nothing can replace face-to-face interaction. Instead of looking at your mobile phone all the time, put it down and look at other people when you are speaking with them. When you look into someone's eyes, you are sending them the message that you recognize their presence and you see them. It feels good to be seen and noticed. You can make brief eye contact with strangers, too. As they walk towards you, acknowledge their existence with your eyes.

You can also practice eye gazing meditation with a friend or partner. Look into each other's eyes for thirty seconds, or up to as long as ten minutes, without speaking or looking away. It might feel uncomfortable the first few times you do this, but this practice will help you develop a deeper connection with others and synchronize your energy with them.

2. Be present.

Being present with another helps create closer bonds. People feel appreciated when you give them your full attention. When interacting with others, make sure your mind is not wandering or distracted and thinking of what to do next, or analyzing the information they share with you. The simple act of listening and being present is enough to offer support and love. You don't have to react to what they say or give them advice.

Reactivity doesn't help you connect with others. If people come to you and complain about their life and you join them in complaining, you only encourage them to think of themselves as victims. On the flip side, if you dismiss their views and try to fix them or give them advice, it might trigger them to justify or defend their position, and this will make you feel frustrated with them.

Being present is none of the above. When you are present, you listen to the other person without reacting to their complaints or judging them. You acknowledge and understand the state they are in. But at the same time, you know that deep down inside they are much more than what they are presenting to you. They are spiritual beings, just like you. With time, they will know who they are, because their inner being will push them in the direction of growth and expansion. There is no need for you to persuade them to change. However, if you choose to respond to another's negativity, you have to come from a place of deep stillness, not from a place of reactivity or trying to convince them to accept your beliefs and way of looking at life.

Being present with another is the same as being present with your mind. Your mind might complain and be judgmental. If you buy into the mind's story and join your mind in complaining, your headspace will get very noisy. On the other hand, if you deny or resist your thoughts, your mind will keep looping the same thoughts. When you are present and mindful of your thoughts, you can simply notice your thoughts and then drop them. When there is space between you (the awareness) and your thoughts, the noise in your head will eventually subside. It's just like how a friend comes to you and complains. If you hold the space for them, they will eventually walk away because they are not getting any reaction from you; or you might help them open up to a deeper dimension within themselves that they were previously unaware of.

3. Recognize the oneness of humanity.

There are moments of connection everywhere. You just have to recognize them. Usually, I don't like crowded places. If the bus or train is crowded, I would rather wait for another one. Then, four years ago, I found myself stuck at a crowded train interchange one day and I had to move along with everyone else. At that time, instead of feeling annoyed, I felt deeply connected and touched. I realized that I'm not just a single drop of water among all the little droplets of water in the ocean. I am the ocean. My sense of self and separation from others dissolved as I moved together with the stream of people.

Previously, I had always focused on how different I am from others. But in essence, I'm just like everyone else. We share the same oxygen in the same room. All of our hearts are beating to keep us alive. They are alive, just as I am alive. This aliveness that both of us possess binds us together. One day, we will evaporate and disappear, but in the end, we will end up back in the same ocean. Our physical forms will die but our spirits are always connected to the same source. Recognizing the oneness of humanity and knowing that we are all in this together, I feel connected.

Now, from time to time, I look at strangers on the train and connect with them spiritually, even though they are doing their own thing and don't realize I'm observing them. You can connect with another person even when the other person is not actively connecting with you. Just see beyond what they are doing and how they are acting, and appreciate their existence. It feels great when you realize that, at this moment, we are on this Earth together at the same place sharing a human experience and we are not alone in this. We are all here to experience love, peace, and expansion.

Even if you and your loved one are physically distant or have a disagreement, you can still have a deep spiritual connection, as long as you recognize how interconnected we are as spirits.

4. Join a spiritual community.

Once you are on a spiritual path, connecting with others on the first three levels might not be as satisfying as they used to be. You will probably be less interested in hanging out with friends who remain at the status quo.

Your friends are familiar with the old you, so they will keep relating to you in the same way. This can hinder the growth of your soul. Your previous friends will either join you in your new level of consciousness or they will distance themselves from you on their own. It feels uncomfortable for two parties, who are vibrating at different levels of energy, to come together and interact with each other for long periods of time, because now you are on different wavelengths. Resonance can exist only if one person decides to increase or decrease their vibration to match the other.

Instead of changing your vibration to match others, most likely, you will have to let these friendships go and cultivate new friendships that are more aligned with you on the spiritual level. Joining a spiritual community might be a better option for your spiritual growth. But you don't have to seek a purely spiritual group. Some of the available groups might be too "woo woo" or New Age for you. What's important is to find groups of people who have some spiritual experience of their own and you can resonate with them energetically. They are people who share the same spiritual knowing as you, who can remind you of your spiritual self and grow with you. Engage with a group of people who bring out the best in each member and learn from each other, a group in which you can explore deeper topics, such as your purpose and contributions in life — not just the common topics that many people are concerned about like careers and relationships.

For example, I am part of a Men's Group in Singapore. Even though it's a group that supports other men with their problems, sometimes we talk about spirituality and do spiritual practices to help us stay present with ourselves and with each other. As long as you are in a group in which everyone can be present, talk from their heart, and listen to each other without judgment, you are in a good space for the soul to emerge and spiritual connection to be developed. But if you want a purely spiritual group, you can always consider looking for such a group, or even start your own.

Conclusion

The Realization We Are Love

When you are feeling lonely, like something or someone is missing, you are really missing your spiritual self, your true essence, the love within. But strictly speaking, nothing is missing. There is no need to reconnect to love because we are love, one and inseparable. We are all striving for the realization that we are love, which is why the regular practice of solitude and meditation is so important. Spiritual practices help remind us of who we are.

Saying "I am love" is more powerful than
saying "I want love."

The statement "I am love" makes love part of your identity. "I want love" suggests you don't have love right now, something is missing. Once you take on the identity of love, everything changes. Instead of trying to get love, you become love and start to think and act from the perspective of love. For example, I often find myself asking: *What would Love do in this situation? Would Love resent or judge other people? Does Love need attention and validation from other people?*

When you become love, you don't need anything else to feel love. You don't need to be more successful, more desirable, or more helpful to be worthy of love. Worthiness is not even a concept you need to consider because there is no condition to love. You can feel love all the time.

When we realize we are love, there can be no loneliness. But if we do feel lonely again, which some of us might… well, it's just another reminder to reconnect to love.

Did You Like *Reconnect to Love*?

Thank you for purchasing my book and spending the time to read it.

Before you go, I'd like to ask you for a small favor. Could you please take a couple of minutes to leave a review for this book on Amazon?

Your feedback will not only help me grow as an author; it will also help those readers who need to hear the message in this book. So, thank you!

Please leave a review at:

http://www.nerdycreator.com/reconnect-to-love.

More Books by Yong Kang

Parent Yourself Again: Love Yourself the Way You Have Always Wanted to Be Loved (Self-Compassion Book 3)

The Disbelief Habit: How to Use Doubt to Make Peace with Your Inner Critic (Self-Compassion Book 2)

Empty Your Cup: Why We Have Low Self-Esteem and How Mindfulness Can Help (Self-Compassion Book 1)

The Emotional Gift: Memoir of a Highly Sensitive Person Who Overcame Depression

Fearless Passion: Find the Courage to Do What You Love

To see the latest books by the author, please go to www.nerdycreator.com/books.

About the Author

Yong Kang Chan, best known as Nerdy Creator, is a blogger, mindfulness teacher, and private tutor. Having low self-esteem growing up, he has read a lot of books on personal growth, psychology, and spirituality.

Based in Singapore, Yong Kang teaches mathematics to his students. On his website, he writes blog posts on self-compassion, mindfulness, and spirituality to help people connect with their deeper dimensions within.

Please visit his website at www.nerdycreator.com.

23149294R00113